Heathrow Cabbie

Heathrow Cabbie

Alf Townsend

First published 2010

The History Press
The Mill, Brimscombe Port
Stroud, Gloucestershire, GL5 2QG
www.thehistorypress.co.uk

© Alf Townsend, 2010

The right of Alf Townsend to be identified as the Author
of this work has been asserted in accordance with the
Copyrights, Designs and Patents Act 1988.

All rights reserved. No part of this book may be reprinted
or reproduced or utilised in any form or by any electronic,
mechanical or other means, now known or hereafter invented,
including photocopying and recording, or in any information
storage or retrieval system, without the permission in writing
from the Publishers.

British Library Cataloguing in Publication Data.
A catalogue record for this book is available from the British Library.

ISBN 978 0 7524 5387 3

Typesetting and origination by The History Press
Printed in Great Britain
Manufacturing managed by Jellyfish Print Solutions Ltd

CONTENTS

ACKNOWLEDGEMENTS

My thanks to my son Nick, a regular cabbie at Heathrow, for bothering to take all the photographs of the taxi shelters, the Knowledge boys and Heathrow. I know I can be a bit of a pain sometimes when I want a certain shot, but Nick understands me.

I must offer my heartfelt thanks also to Mick Rose, another regular cabbie at Heathrow and a fellow author and trade journalist, for supplying me with up-to-date Heathrow anecdotes. Mick wrote a very successful compendium – now in its third print-run – called *The London Cab-Driver's Handbook,* which is a must for every London cabbie. I wasn't to know at the time, but when I contacted him, Mick, his wife Maureen and their family were going through the awful trauma of losing their lovely daughter, still in her twenties and with a young baby. But Mick's response to my request was a clear example of what our trade is *really* about, helping your fellow cabbie if it's within your power to do so! Mick replied that he'd love to help me – just as soon as he got his brain working again. True to his word he supplied me with some amusing anecdotes just a few weeks later. Naturally I appreciate ALL the help that anyone can give me, but in Mick's case it's something special. So thanks a million mate, keep your head up and don't let the bastards grind you down.

My thanks to all my other fellow cabbies for the bits and pieces they supplied me with to help complete the book.

FOREWORD

Alf Townsend has been associated with the London taxi trade press and its politics for as long as I can remember. He is a lifelong member of the LTDA (the Licensed Taxi Drivers Association) and first started writing articles for its flagship publication, *Taxi Newspaper*, way back in the early 1970s. Some years later he was invited to write regular features in the newly launched *Taxi Globe*. He moved on to the *London Taxi Times*, then finally the *Cab Driver*.

In 2007 Alf was invited to return to *Taxi Newspaper* by the LTDA's General Secretary, Bob Oddy, because, as Bob said, 'both I and the executive committee believe he is the best writer in the trade!'

Alf always writes what he believes is the truth and over the years his hard-hitting and down-to-earth comments have often upset many notables in the trade. However, his regular readers enjoy his fortnightly humourous columns that forever cock a snook at the establishment. He has always involved himself in the trade that he loves, being it playing soccer for the taxi team, running the London Marathon for charity or joining the golf society. For ten years he organised all the cab trade golf tournaments, gaining sponsorship from major companies and taking the lucky qualifiers to Spain for a FREE golf holiday in the sun! Alf loves his golf but will be the first to admit that he's rubbish!

Back in 1979, after many unsuccessful attempts, Alf finally won the prestigious Taxi Driver of the Year Competition and managed to promote the trade with a host of appearances on TV game shows and radio interviews.

In the early 1990s, Alf was appointed as Senior LTDA trade representative at Heathrow Airport. Along with all the other trade reps he worked long and hard to form the cabdrivers' co-operative HALT (Heathrow Airport Licensed Taxis), eventually becoming its chairman. Alf then started the *Halt Magazine* and, almost unaided, produced and edited it for the next five-and-a-half years. From its humble beginnings as a six-page black and white effort, the *Halt Magazine* blossomed into a popular, self-sufficient, twenty-page full colour publication.

In the late 1990s, after the tragic loss of his eldest daughter Jenny to breast cancer, Alf decided it was time to give up all his political positions and concentrate on trying to write a book. His first book, *Cabbie*, was published in 2004 and became very successful, so much so that the publishers printed a paperback edition, *The London Cabbie: A Life's Knowledge*, in 2006. In between times, Alf wrote *Bad Lads: RAF National Service Remembered.* This also sold very well over the next two years and in August 2008 Alf made it four in a row when the story of his horrendous life as an evacuee in the Second World War was published entitled *Blitz Boy*. Thanks to the support of many of his cab-trade readers, this book sold nearly 1,000 copies in the first week of publication. Alf's next book – number five, published in 2009 – was called *The Black Cab Story* and traced the longevity of the famous London taxi trade way back to 1654 and Oliver Cromwell, who was indeed the founding father of our trade!

This book, *Heathrow Cabbie*, will hopefully be equally as successful!

Stuart Pessok
Editor, TAXI

INTRODUCTION

Following the initial success of my first book, *Cabbie*, and the paperback follow up, *The London Cabbie: A Life's Knowledge*, it would have been as easy as shelling peas to knock out a *Cabbie Two* book in double-quick time – especially with all my many years in the trade. Incidentally, my sincere apologies to many of my readers who wrongly purchased the paperback thinking it was a new book. All we did was redesign the jacket cover and I finally got my own way when the publishers decided to change the title back to my original choice. I hope I can placate all those irate readers who telephoned the publishers having a good scream about the paperback by paraphrasing an old, and very wise, saying – 'You can't tell a book by its cover!'

The round-the-world advertising following the opening of Terminal 5 in March 2008 – closely followed by the mother of all PR disasters for BAA – led me to start delving into the long history of the actual Heathrow site. And it really is a long history, going right back to the last Ice Age when the south-east of England was underwater and, after the water subsided, the gravel deposited made the ground perfect for a future international airport!

The following centuries revealed an amazing amount of interesting facts culminating in the government's decision in 1943 to select Heathrow as London's post-war airport. Following the recent release of sensitive documents from that time, it would appear that the government's use of emergency wartime powers in this particular instance, (*The Defence Of The Realm Act, 1939*), was in fact a not-quite-legal ploy to push their decision through without any hassle – and with no right of appeal whatsoever!

The inauguration by HRH Queen Elizabeth II of the first terminal building in 1955, then called the Queen's Buildings or Terminal 1 (but now known as Terminal 2), heralded the arrival of London's licensed taxis on the scene. This followed an Act of Parliament allowing taxis to ply for hire at the newly opened 'London Airport Heathrow'.

All these different facets of Heathrow's history – coupled with a myriad of anecdotal stories about London's famous cabbies that I have collected after working Heathrow for a decade – made me decide that this was not just going to be another cabbie book and not just the story of Heathrow. I shall attempt to weave both fascinating stories together and make it an interesting read for both passengers and cabbies alike. It is not my intention to deliberately plagiarise my first book *Cabbie*, but I need to use some of those facts again to ensure continuity.

Alf Townsend
Hampstead, 2010

1

BACK TO THE BEGINNING

In the present day, Heathrow is the world's busiest airport and its second busiest cargo port. It is the UK's largest airport, employing in excess of 60,000 workers, and carries some 90 million passengers every year, despite Terminal 5's (T5) opening shambles of mislaying 28,000 pieces of luggage!

Anyone in today's modern world walking around the vast expanse of Heathrow, seeing all the many thousands of passengers scurrying about – plus the unending noise of massive planes taking off and landing over eighteen unbroken hours – would find it almost impossible to fully comprehend the humble beginnings of this massive, international airport.

The foundations of Heathrow's place in our history were laid some 25 million years ago when south-east England became submerged under the sea. A flat layer of gravel was deposited around 14 miles west of what is now Trafalgar Square and, when the waters subsided, it was this flatness and the excellent drainage characteristics of the gravel that eventually made it the perfect site for an airport.

Man's place in the landscape of Heathrow has been traced back to a Romano-Celtic temple excavated in 1944, and all pottery discovered on the site dates back to 300BC. In Roman times, Hounslow Heath was a deep forest through which a

Roman road ran from London to what is now Staines, and then on to the West Country.

In the thirteenth century, King Henry III cleared the deep forest to create a heath for the purpose of hunting; and on this heath over the years developed a hamlet known variously throughout the centuries as Hetherewe, Hetherow, Hedrowe and Heath Row.

By the seventeenth century, the muddy and treacherous road across the open heathland – used continuously by stagecoaches travelling between London and the West Country – became the favourite haunt of highwaymen. Strange to relate, but the most notorious of these highwaymen was in fact a 'highway lady' called Moll Cutpurse. She led a gang of audacious robbers who terrorised stagecoach passengers for many months before the law caught up with them. Many of them were captured and hanged at Tyburn Tree, a site very close to where Marble Arch now stands. Their remains were brought back to Hounslow Heath and the grisly parts were hung on gibbets, just to deter any other would-be highwaymen! According to local legend, the area was also frequented by the 'King' of highwaymen Dick Turpin, who is rumoured to have hidden from the law behind a fireplace in the Green Man Tavern at Hatton. Old Dick must have had a very fit nag because the local legend in my 'manor', Hampstead, was that he was very active on Hampstead Heath – over 20 miles from Hatton – hence the pub by his name in Spaniard's Road!

During the eighteenth century, Hounslow Heath became a popular dawn rendezvous for gentlemen duellists, out to settle their differences with swords or pistols. Later it was utilised by the army for drill, exercises and parades.

In 1784, the flatness of the Heathrow area and its proximity to London and the Royal Observatory at Greenwich made it the perfect site for the original base mark of the world's very first ordnance survey. I have always found the facts of this particular operation fascinating. Out of the blue, up turns

Major General William Roy and his troop of engineers. They hammered in wooden pikes at Heathrow and at the 'poor house' at Hampton Hill to the south amd joined the pikes with a line. Then a second line was created from Hanger Hill, Ealing, in the east, to St Anne's Hill, Chertsey, in the west, which crossed the first line. From these two lines, Roy not only made up the first two triangles of England's very first ordnance survey, but he also began the first international system that was to reach across France and on to the farthest corners of the earth. His original wooden pikes at Heathrow were replaced by an upright cannon which was moved to the site of the old taxi feeder park in 1944, during the airport's construction. Back in the 1980s when the cabbies were asked to choose a name for the new canteen in their brand-new taxi feeder park – scheduled to be opened by Linda Lusardi, the then voluptuous Page Three model – many cabbies, myself included, plumped for the name 'General Roy's' in memory of the old army engineer's foresight.

Heathrow's eventual place in aviation history can be traced back to the First World War when the army used nearby Hounslow Heath as a training aerodrome for the Royal Flying Corps. In response to a possible threat of bombs from Zeppelin airships, a crescent of aerodromes was built around the south of London, with Hounslow Heath becoming the headquarters. It remained a military airfield until 1919 when it became the first 'Customs' airport for London. However, by the 1920s Hounslow Heath had lost this early lead in civil aviation to the airport at Croydon.

The old adage saying that, 'nothing is cast in stone,' became very true because, by the time the Second World War was well into its third year, the hunt was now on for a military aerodrome suitable for long-term expansion; it had to also be capable of handling Tiger Force, the new longer-range bombers, and the massive military transport aircraft that were needed to resupply our troops in Burma and

Malaya. So, once again the pecking order changed! Pressure was also mounting on the government to find a suitable site for London's new civil airport when the war was over, but they needed to tread very carefully over this issue.

Croydon Airport fell at the first hurdle as it was considered inappropriate for future expansion because it was built on a hill and surrounded by urban sprawl. Hounslow Heath and 'The Great West Aerodrome', a 150-acre site in the area of Heathrow Village, purchased in 1927 by Fairey Aviation – pioneers of aircraft flaps which increase lift and/or drag at low speed – became the clear favourite. One of the main reasons why this area eventually got the vote as the site for the new London airport was quite simple: it could be done with the minimum amount of fuss or disturbance to householders, because at that time Heathrow was surrounded on all sides by market gardens.

By the end of 1943, and after much discussion, a Cabinet committee finally decided that London's new post-Second World War airport should be Heathrow. Speaking about the decision, Civil Aviation Minister Lord Winster said, 'Our main interest lies in ensuring that as many as possible of the colonies are served by one or more of the main trunk routes and are thus provided by speedy means of communication with the mother country and with other parts of the empire.' He went on, 'The site is only some twelve miles from London. The land is remarkably level and the gravel sub-soil has excellent bearing and drainage qualities . . . To meet the need for a major air terminal to serve London, fifty-two sites were surveyed. No better site for the purpose could be found than Heathrow.' The government, using emergency wartime powers (*The Defence Of The Realm Act, 1939*), instantly drew up a compulsory purchase order in 1944. Evidence has since emerged indicating that using emergency wartime powers to push this deal through without any hassle, and with no right of appeal whatsoever, was not an entirely legal ploy.

Even the official version depicting the origins of Heathrow doesn't quite stand up to scrutiny with the new evidence emerging today. Firstly, the premise that it was originally developed as a military airfield for the RAF in the Second World War, able to function as the supply base for the Tiger Force, and that it naturally evolved into the main civil airport for London at the end of the war is not quite so clear-cut. In fact, the release of certain, once-sensitive documents under the Freedom of Information Act, have shown that in reality this was far from the truth! In his autobiography published in 1973 and entitled *Wings Over Westminster*, Harold Balfour, (later Lord Balfour of Inchrye) who was Parliamentary Under-Secretary of State between 1938 and 1944, stated that he 'deceived' the Cabinet committees over the requisitioning of land for post-war aviation needs. Why should he bother to do that, you may ask? Let me lay out the scenario for you. It is 1943 and the government would have been crucified if it was discovered that they wanted to divert urgent resources away from the war effort at such a crucial time simply to build a post-war civil airport! London was still under attack from Hitler's terror weapons, the V1s and V2s – 'V' was for 'Vengeance'. This was Hitler's last throw of the dice in an effort to secure peace talks. Preparations were still being made for Operation Overlord, the massive Allied invasion of Europe. However, Balfour persisted in making a strong and lengthy case for the need to requisition land at Heathrow, stressing that it was imperative for our troops in the Far East that we have a long-range bomber airfield to supply them. But strangely, he failed to inform his fellow cabinet colleagues of the many suitable airfields already available in the Home Counties. Balfour eventually persuaded the Cabinet, and the government took the land. They informed Middlesex County Council on 31 May that a compulsory purchase order had been drawn up. The Air Ministry acquired 2,800 acres, excluding the original Hounslow Heath Customs and

Military Airfield. However, the purchase order did include the hamlet Heath Row and the Great West Aerodrome. Fairey Aviation moved to the nearby Heston Aerodrome.

Balfour had finally got his way and the deal had been done. However, the government subterfuge was set to continue, as you will discover in the following chapter.

2

LONDON AIRPORT HEATHROW IS BORN

Later in 1943, on 6 June, work began on the runways. To maintain the government's deception of it being developed for the RAF, a runway was built that was totally unsuitable for civil purposes and which was subsequently and conveniently abandoned without ever having been used! In point of fact, the RAF never used the airport and the very first flight in early 1946 was a civil flight which took place purely for publicity purposes; *Star Light*, a British South American Airways (BSAA) Avro Lancastrian aircraft, (a converted Lancaster bomber), took off on a long-distance proving flight to Buenos Aires. It was carrying six crew and just ten passengers – including a BBC reporter and company officials who would operate the South American end of the service – plus a ton of mail. After stopping twice for refuelling and fighting strong headwinds and tropical rainstorms, *Star Light* finally reached Buenos Aires a staggering 35 hours after leaving Heathrow! How flight times have improved over sixty-odd years!

However, by 1947 the protests against Heathrow were getting louder and louder. An overly dramatic article in the *Middlesex Advertiser & Gazette* of the same year stated, 'An atomic bomb dropped at Heathrow could not spread devastation more widely than the disruption caused by the construction of an airport on this spot.' These protests against the expansion of Heathrow would rumble on for decades as each new terminal was built in the central area and even more surrounding land was gobbled up by BAA. The protests reached a crescendo when, in 1978, a public inquiry was set up to investigate plans to build Terminal 4 on the opposite side of the airport. Suddenly the protesters realised that BAA weren't satisfied with their expansion in the central area and virtually any part of their now almost 3,000 acres, could be used eventually for new terminals. A certain Mr Glidewell, the inspector of the T4 public inquiry, was accredited with these immortal words in his closing speech before basically rubber-stamping the T4 proposal, 'I am strongly of the opinion that all possible steps should be taken to satisfy those living around Heathrow that this is THE LAST MAJOR EXPANSION.' Even in 1983, when the first feelers were being put out about the need for a fifth terminal, BAA stated, 'There are multiple risks associated with a fifth terminal . . . they add up to a total risk which is completely unacceptable.'

However, despite fierce opposition – not only from local residents but people living under the flight paths and from powerful organisations like Friends of the Earth, too – in November 2001 the Secretary of State finally approved the construction of Terminal 5. It turned out to be the longest public inquiry in British history (46 months) and the planning process itself cost nearly £63m over a period of 14 years. The cost was borne mostly by BAA and BA, the two main proponents of the project.

~

At Heathrow in 1946 an RAF triangular pattern of runways was adopted to allow take-offs in any wind direction. However, a committee later decided to develop the original pattern into a double-triangle 'Star of David' to permit parallel take-offs and landings in any wind direction. Heathrow's two major runways today, 1 and 5, are based on the original north and south sides of the two triangles, and its 'cross-wind' runway is the original transverse Runway 2. Because the original Runway 3 was close to the central terminal area, an additional parallel strip was developed as Runway 7.

The formal title, 'London Airport Heathrow', was adopted from 25 March 1946, and on the wet blustery morning of the 28 March, a British Overseas Airways Corporation (BOAC) Avro Lancastrian took off on the 'Kangaroo Run' to Sydney. Lancastrians normally took up to thirteen passengers, but the need to install bunks on this exceptionally long service reduced the capacity to just six. Each passenger had an armchair, window and table! The very first aircraft to land at the new airport was a BOAC Lancastrian from Australia, quickly followed by Lockheed Constellation airliners of Pan Am and American Overseas Airways.

Soon after the war ended the Labour government nationalised civil aviation to bring all airports and aerodromes in the UK under the control of the new Ministry of Civil Aviation. They even nationalised the airlines as well and created three very large airway corporations: BOAC, serving Commonwealth, North America and Far Eastern destinations; BSAA, flying to South America; and British European Airways (BEA), flying domestic and short-haul routes into Europe.

The main emphasis was to get the runways laid and make Heathrow fully operational. By 1947 three runways had been completed – at the expense of no terminal buildings whatsoever. A tented village was set up on the north side of the airport with a row of red telephone boxes and a mobile post office alongside the hastily erected tents. Inside, the tents were furnished with comfortable chintz armchairs and had a bar, a WH Smith & Son, a Cable & Wireless desk and Elsan toilets. However, 1947 saw a very wet summer and fire buckets were used to catch the rain and duckboards placed to protect passengers from the thick oozing mud! Later in the year, these tents were eventually replaced by a series of ex-military, pre-fabricated buildings. These ugly buildings on the North Side remained until the early 1990s.

In 1961 Terminal 3 was completed for the long-haul flights. In 1966, BAA was created because of increasing government bureaucracy. They were in control of Heathrow, Gatwick, Stansted and Prestwick near Glasgow, but BAA remained government-owned until privatisation took place in 1987. After BAA was first created, 1967 saw the opening of the new short-haul terminal (now T1) for UK airline services although it wasn't formally opened by the queen until 17 April 1969. Then, in September 1970, Concorde, the world's very first supersonic jet airliner, landed at Heathrow for the first time on a diversion from Farnborough. In January 1976, British Airways introduced Concorde supersonic services at Heathrow simultaneously with Air France in Paris.

The tunnel, which provides the main road access to the central terminal area, was opened in 1955. Again, with the benefit of hindsight, this tunnel has proved to be a flawed concept. It struggles to cope with today's massive flow of airport traffic and any breakdowns or accidents in the tunnel can – and have – brought the airport to a complete standstill. Many security experts are concerned that the strategic importance of the tunnel to the smooth running of Heathrow could make it a prime target for any terrorist bomber.

The so-called 'expert' planners had also got their car-parking calculations for the central area all wrong. In their dear, old-fashioned English way, they had wrongly assumed that civil aviation in the future would only be the prerogative of the very rich and famous. They wrongly assumed that all these toffs would arrive in chauffeur-driven limousines and simply check in after a smart salute from their employees! In effect, their thinking was that not one of these people would ever require parking spaces. It was a costly error and a waste of many thousands of man-hours over the years as people were gridlocked in their cars in the central area. The problem was temporarily solved by the hasty erection of multi-storey car parks for each terminal in the central area. Again with the benefit of hindsight, the erection of these multi-storey car parks proved to be another mistake because, instead of pushing for the public transport option, they encouraged passengers and friends to come in their cars – thus increasing congestion even more!

As the years rolled by and Heathrow became even busier, the increased congestion in the central area became an everyday nightmare. Despite constant and volatile demonstrations, this never-ending traffic chaos led to the birth of Terminal 4 in 1986. The new terminal was built on the south side of the airport, a very modern facility for sure, with a price tag of £22m. However, it had the drawback of being an inconvenient 5-mile transfer from the central area around already congested perimeter roads.

3

THE NEW TERMINAL 5

After a four-year public inquiry came the final piece in the massive Heathrow jigsaw: the construction of Terminal 5. This was a truly, multi-billion pound project – expected to cost £4.2billion and funded entirely by BAA and not the taxpayer. This massive build was finally completed in March 2008 although it isn't expected to be until 2013 that all the phases of the project will be complete.

Archaeologists, allowed on to the site during the excavations, found evidence of human activity dating back to the Stone Age, with 80,000 objects including 18,000 pieces of pottery, 40,000 pieces of worked flint and the only wooden bowl ever found that dates back to the Middle Bronze Age. They have also found evidence to suggest that field boundaries at Heathrow were in place from 2,000BC – some 500 years earlier than previously thought.

During the build on the old sludge works of Perry Oaks to the west of the central area, T5 was Europe's largest building site, employing some 6,500 people and seeing a fully-laden lorry enter the site every 31 seconds. Spending was running at a peak rate of £4m a day. The main building (or T5A) is 400m long, 180m wide and 43m high – the same height as Tower Bridge. The total area covered by T5 is 265 hectares – as large as Hyde Park, or four times as big as T4. You could fit fifty football pitches in the massive structure with around ten pitches to each of its five floors. T5 contains 105 lifts, 65 escalators and has 80,000 tonnes of steel – with 17,000 tonnes in the roof of T5A alone.

T5A and T5B (and later T5C) are connected by an underground people-mover, which can transfer passengers between the two in 50 seconds and 13.5km of tunnels connect the terminal into the Piccadilly Line and Heathrow Express.

Terminal 5 will serve around 30 million passengers a year, eventually taking the number of people Heathrow serve every year to a massive 90 million! The 87m high control tower is double the height of the present Heathrow tower and is the tallest in the UK. When completed, the centrepiece of the new terminal will be an open-air plaza between the passenger arrival points and the terminal. The plaza will be almost 400 metres long, with mature plane trees, fountains and cafés. At each end there will be glass artworks by Ben Langlands and Nikki Bell, inscribed with the three-letter codes of the world's airports, such as LHR (London Heathrow) and JFK (John F. Kennedy Airport in New York) .

Despite all the billions of pounds spent on its construction, things went decidedly pear-shaped after its grand opening by the queen in March 2008. In fact it became a veritable PR disaster for the following month or so as their much-publicised automatic baggage delivery system broke down completely and some 28,000 pieces of luggage went astray! Experts have since said that the grand opening was rushed and that the system hadn't been trialled sufficiently. BAA certainly got plenty of advertising all over the world but not exactly the kind of advertising they wanted!

As part of the long-running inquiry into T5, concerns were expressed regarding the impact on the environment from such a massive building project. BAA have had to give careful consideration to this and around 20,000 trees and shrubs have been planted and the landscaping includes many plants which are native to the area. Even the two rivers, the Longford and the Duke of Northumberland – which used to run directly through the sewage treatment works – have been diverted to run along the perimeter, thus creating an improved environment.

Heathrow has come an awfully long way since its far-off days as a hamlet on a blustery heath and its peaceful pre-war days as a haven for market gardens. However, many local people are deeply concerned about the loss of their ancient villages and the possible loss of their loved ones laying at rest in the local graveyards. They question whether the building of T5 was really necessary despite BAA suggesting that Heathrow would decline and lose status to other major European airports if T5 had not been built. Protesters say that in fact, 'The only competition between airports is for people changing planes. These are a minority of passengers who bring extra noise and pollution, but who contribute little to the UK economy because they are only passing through on their way elsewhere.' They argue that much of T5 will be just a vast shopping centre with more retail space than Staines (the nearest town) – not because these shops are needed by local people, but because BAA make more profits from retail and duty-free sales to passengers than from airlines. BAA's counter argument is that without T5 the annual number of passengers would be 30,000 fewer, seeing a vastly smaller passenger volume number of 54 million rather than nearly 90 million.

Friends of the Earth released a damning seven-page briefing that highlighted the many dangers to the environment with the possible building of T5 and a third runway. Their briefing undoubtedly packed a punch and their evidence was certainly convincing. They explained how the Heathrow site is now close to 3,000 acres and that the tarmac area alone is equivalent to 200 miles of three-lane motorways. They also provided an in-depth analysis about the air pollution in West London being full of toxic cocktails served up by aircraft, motorways and local roads. They continued with how Heathrow operates 24 hours a day, all year long and they quoted the words from BAA in February 1983, 'There are multiple risks associated with a fifth terminal . . . they add up to a total risk which is completely unacceptable.' They believed that the building of T5 is only one step away from building a third runway. They quoted former Deputy Prime Minister and Secretary of State for the Environment John Prescott, who in the *Observer* in February 1993 said, 'There will ultimately be more flights over the most congested airway in Europe, at great cost to the environment and to congestion around the airport.'

Journalists picked up on the briefing with one writing, 'I feel a sense of irrational unease at the spectacle of airports relying so much on shopping for such a large slice of their income instead of air travel.' Another wrote about importing more cargo, 'And does eating strawberries in December represent a significant advance in civilisation?'

Friends of the Earth concluded their 'BAA bashing' briefing by accusing all and sundry of 'vested interests'. Sadly, the powers-that-be completely ignored all of these compelling facts and simply went ahead with T5's construction.

But does T5 really mark the end of expansion plans at Heathrow? Apparently not, because at the time of writing, and despite years of vociferous protests, the government has agreed to the building of a third runway. Whispers are beginning to circulate that even a sixth terminal could be on the cards for the future! The business community have convinced the politicians that a third runway is absolutely imperative for the financial future of Britain. They argue that if we allow other major European airports like Frankfurt, Charles de Gaulle or Schiphol to overtake Heathrow, then the City will lose its place as the financial capital of the world. This in turn, they say, could well have a drastic effect on our future economy. Many others argue that this is expansion purely for the sake of profit and has nothing whatsoever to do with the UK's financial future. The findings of a well-known statistician make for interesting reading. His results seem to indicate that a third runway and a possible sixth terminal will do nothing to improve the economy whatsoever!

What about the many hundreds of local people whose lives will be upturned by compulsory purchase orders slapped on their homes? The ancient village of Sipson – just across the road from the airport – is a prime example. This proposed third runway is planned to run directly through the existing village, virtually wiping it off the map forever as 700 homes and a school will be demolished and there are plans to build a dual carriageway right through the cemetery in Cherry Lane. So, not only will the poor residents of Sipson be forced to vacate their homes, but even their departed loved ones will have to be raised from their resting places and reinterred elsewhere. In a recent TV interview, a BAA spokesperson refuted the suggestion that they are going to build a road through the Cherry Lane Cemetery. He said, 'this idea was only on the provisional map that has now been changed and updated.'

BAA have gone out of their way to convince the residents – and the rest of the country – that they will pay the 2003 going rate for the properties plus 10 per cent and removal costs. However, money simply cannot make up for the heartache of a CPO because many generations of the same families were born and grew up in the village. When you break up a community you ruin many lives forever. Hopefully for the people of Sipson, all these future plans could well turn out to be purely hypothetical, because if Labour loses the 2010 election – as is looking highly likely at the present time – then the Conservatives have already stated that they will scrap the plans for a third runway.

The experts predict a massive rise in the numbers of people flying within the next decade – almost double the present numbers some say. The obvious answer is to build more airports in the south of England or more runways and more terminals on existing sites. My reply to those questions from residents living close to Heathrow is yes, unfortunately there WILL be more runways and terminals in the future.

4

LONDON TAXIS ARRIVE AT HEATHROW

Following the inauguration of the first terminal in 1955 by the queen, an act of parliament was passed which allowed London taxis to ply for hire at Heathrow. The world-famous London cabbies had received their very first ordinance from Oliver Cromwell in 1654 in *The Regulation for ye Betterment of ye Hackney Coachmen in London*. The rules laid down by Cromwell are basically the same as those which cabbies have to abide by today. Only Ken Livingstone, the former Mayor of London, broke the longevity of the rules when he increased the legal distance a cab could be hired from 6 to 12 miles. In hindsight, I reckon Ken got it right for once, especially when one realises the 6-mile limit was imposed in 1642 – not to prevent the old horse getting too tired, as many people believe, but to protect the Hackney coachmen from going beyond the chain of defences built 6 miles around London during the English Civil War of 1642. Incidentally for all you history buffs, the word 'Hackney' has got nothing whatsoever to do with the London borough of that name. It comes from a Flemish term *'Haquenué'* which means, 'A dappled grey horse that originally came from Flanders.'

This ancient ordinance has been renewed by parliament every year since. Some 350 years later and the cabbies were starting to ply their trade at the world-famous Heathrow Airport.

In the early days the cabbies consisted of a small group of hardy souls who were happy to face the daily search for a minute number of fares from just one terminal. The cabbies were parked up on the North Side among the Nissen huts and the hastily laid cinder, and had to abide by a primitive ticket system, totally unfair and controlled by a policeman. One particular policeman was a bit of a character, or so I am told. He was very fair and considerate to all the cabbies and went by the strange nickname of 'Woodentop'. During my research, I asked one of the old regulars who had worked Heathrow from the year dot, about how he had attained his strange nickname. It appeared, according to this guy, that 'Woodentop' was a bit thick. One day he was instructed by his inspector to park himself by the tunnel entrance and divert all the traffic around the Perimeter Road, to allow a clear access for one of the royals – he believes it may have been the late Princess Margaret. But, as the story goes, being a bit thick he even managed to divert the royal car around the Perimeter Road as well!

It's fair to say that back in the 'bad old days' of dog-eat-dog way before the time of any taxi feeder park and fully-computerised taxi movements – the actual flow of taxis at Heathrow relied purely on the whims and vested interests of small groups of cabbies who organised themselves into cartels or gangs. If my memory serves me right I believe one 'firm' was called 'The Quality Street Gang' and another was 'The Lavender Hill Mob'! If you weren't a member of one of these 'firms' then, ticket or no ticket, you simply couldn't get on the only terminal rank at the then Terminal 1 (now Terminal 2), because when one cab got hired, they would simply leave a space in the middle, only pulling forward when one of their gang appeared. Consequently all the 'Connaughts' (Connaught Rangers – strangers) were forced to continually orbit, that is, circle the central area hoping in vain to find a space. The cartels virtually controlled the rank by not leaving the 'point' (head of the rank) unless it was a good fare that suited them. The choice fares of that era, so I am told, were the groups of Asian immigrants entering the country. All these poor people had in their possession was an address of their contact somewhere up north, maybe in Birmingham, Wolverhampton or Bradford. The guys would load their cabs to overflowing – because their contact would pay 'per head' – then take them to these addresses all over the country. Unfortunately these poor souls had to work like dogs for many months to repay the over-inflated cost of their taxi ride and became virtual slaves to their employers.

Another choice fare that I personally found distressing were all the young foreign girls looking for an abortion in the one country in Europe where it was legal. The guys knew all the addresses where they would receive a fat commission for what was known loosely in Heathrow taxi terminology as 'Belly-Jobs'. But as a loving father of two daughters, it's not my humour, I am simply relating the facts.

If the guy on the 'point' didn't fancy a certain job, or it was a 'local', he would send it to the back of the rank. The guy at the back of the rank who took a 'local' was allowed back on the rank by the cartel – despite all the many cabbies orbiting or waiting over on the North Side.

It was painfully obvious to BAA and just about everybody else that an international airport like Heathrow couldn't possibly function in a professional way with a taxi operation like the one which was in place – especially following some bitter complaints from some very influential and powerful people who had the misfortune of wanting to go on short journeys of no value and finding the cabs simply wouldn't take them. I believe the actress/singer Petula Clark had a right scream up after being turned down for a 'local' and even the late Bobby Kennedy, then the powerful Attorney

General of the USA, who was in transit and wanted to go to a Catholic church in Hounslow for a Sunday service, was given 'a blank'! These complaints had the effect of forcing BAA to urgently sort out a fair and sensible taxi operation. Their first attempt was using what is now the bus depot in the central area as a taxi feeder rank, but it didn't work because it wasn't big enough. Finally, after the opening of T3 in 1961 to cater for long-haul flights and the opening of the now T1 in 1969 for short-haul UK airline services, BAA needed to get their act together because hundreds of taxis were arriving to rank up. They finally utilised some spare space out on the Northern Perimeter Road, bang opposite the Heathrow police station and adjacent to all the old Nissen huts. However, that's when all the trouble and the eventual boycott started. The BAA, out of the blue, suddenly informed the trade organisations that they would be levying an entry charge on each and every taxi entering the new feeder park. Even though the suggested original charge was only a nominal 50p, the drivers and their organisations were furious, telling BAA in no uncertain terms that they supplied a service for THEIR passengers who had already paid exorbitant landing charges for the privilege of arriving at Heathrow. Many of the wiser old heads realised that a nominal 50p charge might well be the thin end of the wedge – with the distinct possibility of an increase every year. How right they were! The entry charge in 2010 had risen to a whopping £5.50p. The cabbies can recover part of this charge with a fare within the Metropolitan Police District (MPD), by putting £2 on the meter as extras – so the poor old Heathrow passenger pays yet again!

The battle lines were drawn with neither side willing to compromise or negotiate. The cabbies were adamant: withdraw the charge at once, or they would withdraw their labour! And so the boycott began, with various volunteers (mostly TGWU members) picketing the entrance to the feeder park. The support from the cabbies was almost total, with just a few scabs ignoring the pickets. After about thirteen weeks and with a judicial review about to be heard (and a possible result going the cabbies' way), they received a body-blow from within. The general secretary of one of the largest trade bodies, for reasons best known to himself, stated that he would be instructing his members to use the new feeder park facility WHATEVER the outcome of the judicial review. That was enough to make the cabbies think long and hard about their endeavour. What was the point of continuing the picket if hundreds of cabbies were going to drive through? The strike crumbled and after more than three months, BAA had won. Again, with the benefit of hindsight, I honestly think we could have won if we had held out for another couple of weeks. The BAA had been receiving bundles of complaints from influential passengers about the continual lack of taxis at Heathrow and questions were even being asked in parliament! The BAA was definitely wobbling and they might well have decided to cut and run within a short space of time.

Over the ensuing years, BAA have installed a workable system in the taxi feeder park that could accommodate over 400 cabs. Mind you, the system was far from perfect and many scallywags concocted all sorts of weird and wonderful ideas to beat it. One such invention was what the boys called the 'two-cab shuffle'. Those involved in the scam would arrive bright and early in the morning, book their cabs into the feeder park and, after about an hour, make a beeline for the exit where their wives or another gang member would be parked up in a second cab. This second cab would be duly booked in and the scallywags sat waiting for their first group to be called up. Assuming it was a straight-forward trip into central London, they would have plenty of time to return, book in once again and simply wait for their second cab to be called up! If, perchance, their scam went a little pear-shaped because of maybe an extra-long fare or being delayed on their return by heavy traffic, then no problems. They simply went to the exit box and made up some cock-and-bull story about being delayed in the loo with a gippy tummy or some other feeble excuse! Come the end of the day those on the 'two-cab shuffle' would be doing twice as many rides as their mates!

The taxi feeder park in those far-off days – especially in the hot summers – was akin to a seaside holiday camp or even the Costa del Sol! The rules and regulations were, at the best, very lax and, at the worst, almost non-existent. The company which ran the feeder park in those days was APCOA, the giant airport parking firm, and, as just employees, they were quite happy to book cabs in and out with not too many questions asked in-between! With laxity, consequently, you get abuse of the system. On any fine summer's day you had a cabbie nicknamed 'Poodles' standing outside the canteen flogging sports gear from a questionable source. This driver got his nickname because he always carried his two poodles in the front of the cab with him on night work. Other guys were wandering about wearing shorts and carrying sets of golf clubs and tennis racquets, waiting for their mates to pick them up. Some drivers who lived locally would meander out to where their wives were waiting in the car and simply go shopping for a couple of hours! The official Heathrow Taxi football, cricket and golf teams were all allowed out to play their matches and then got a ticket down to the terminals immediately on their return without waiting. This generous concession was obviously abused by some hangers-on who got on the weekly freebie bandwagon by posing as 'assistant trainers' complete with buckets, not forgetting the 'goal-keeping coaches' and the groups of 'physios', all wearing white coats and carrying important-looking 'medical equipment' that would be urgently required.

The overall summer scenario in the vast feeder park was very continental to say the least with row after row of half-naked cabbies, heavily oiled, reclining on sun beds and deckchairs and enjoying the midday sun! Sadly their scenic idyll was due to end very shortly when BAA introduced some stringent new bye-laws and it was left to the local 'Gestapo' units to interpret them in their own peculiar way. Following their interpretations of the new bye-laws, one of the guys said to me sorrowfully, the tears noticeable on his sun oil, 'I'll tell you what, Alf, this feeder park is now worse than being in the bleedin' nick. There ain't no parole – once you're in you've got to do your full time!'

I suppose you've got to have bye-laws to make the place run properly, but the problem is the little bloody 'Hitlers' who go strictly by the book and, using these rules, tend to come to ridiculous conclusions. Take bye-law number six for starters, which said, 'No person shall leave his taxi on an authorised standing or taxi feeder rank, or portion thereof, unless willing to be hired immediately.' Now any reasonable person would say, okay, so that puts the kybosh on leaving your cab in the park while you're out doing your thing for a couple of hours, fair enough. But the local 'Fuzz' certainly didn't read it that way. Legend has it that they frog-marched geezers out of the canteen for leaving their cabs unattended, while others swear that a special snatch team had been seen bursting into the bog and dragging other poor unfortunates over to the nick – with their trousers still at half-mast! I reckon you can take those legends with a pinch of salt – or even a couple of pieces of toilet paper.

Even the poor old card players suffer from this bye-law as well. Some say they've been forced to form up their four cabs in line abreast and, from the driving seats, shout out the number on the cards they are throwing. This has come to be known as 'Four Pack Feeder Park Kalooki'!

Even the avid sun worshippers have had to lay their plans in advance to beat the 'Fuzz'. Their cunning plan to stay within the bye-law was exposing their head and shoulders from the driving seat in the morning with and a touch of the hairy legs out of the windows for the afternoon session!

Bye-law number ten stated, 'No person shall wash down or clean out a taxi on an authorised standing.' Now all the guys reckoned that meant a terminal rank, but the local gendarmerie reckoned it included the feeder park as well. Word has it that they sent in plain-clothes officers to try and spot any cabbie trying to empty an ash tray, or craftily wiping over a dirty window! Rumour has it that they posted another 'plank of wood' next to the water taps and, God help the poor ignorant cabbie who dared to appear with an empty bucket!

Bye-law number eleven was a bit of a joke as well. This corker says, 'Taxi drivers who are for the time being on a taxi feeder rank, shall comply with such directions for ensuring good order.' Now this is basically an open invitation for the 'Gestapo' to bloody-well ban just about everything! It's a bit like our old 'friend' that supersedes any of the Hackney Carriage Laws: 'at the discretion of the Commissioner (Police)'. Oh yes, our 'friends' loved this little beauty because it could cover a multitude of sins like, no swearing, no gambling, no politics and no telling Irish, Jewish, Black, Green or Yellow jokes. The penalty for breaking ANY rule that ensures good order? Instant dismissal from the feeder park! They are purging one of the guys at the moment who, unfortunately, has a rather loud 'north and south' (mouth) and does plenty of 'Lord Mayoring' (swearing). He's been in and out of the park all week and I don't think he's done a ride yet!

Bye-law number eleven (A) stated, 'Taxis must leave the feeder park in the order in which they entered.' This is quite a sensible bye law if it is interpreted correctly, but God forbid if you have an airlock, a flat battery, a flat tyre, you've fallen asleep or you've been caught short. Or even if you're having an epileptic fit – or even a heart attack! There's no excuse sunshine, you have lost your place and you either go round again or they carry you out 'brown bread' (dead) if the heart attack was fatal!

So you finally reach the exit box having been the model of discretion and, surprisingly, you haven't waited too long – the reason being that many of the blokes who were in front of you have been slung out of the park for some misdemeanour or another and are now behind you. But I know I'm in trouble when the geezer in the exit box gives me a perishing look because he's recognised me as the mouthy trade journalist who's been writing nasty things about the people who run the feeder park. I know full well that he's going to get me by hitting me with bye-law number thirteen. I quote that when you've given up your ticket at the specified terminal, 'taxi-drivers shall not subsequently transfer their taxis to any other authorised standing unless the consent of a constable or traffic warden in uniform has first been obtained.' I know full well that Terminals 1, 2 and 4 are busy and I know full well that this guy is going to lumber me with a ticket to Terminal 3. He knows and I know that there isn't a flight landing at Terminal 3 for a couple of hours. The baleful face appears once more at the window and, with a sneer, he hands me a ticket.

On my way over to T3 – I told you so – I start to contemplate my predicament. I know full well I'm going to have to roast for at least a couple of hours and I also know that they would have posted a particularly nauseating specimen of a copper on the rank. And I know that this copper is going to be the biggest 'plank of wood' in the whole timber yard and my request for a transfer will be greeted with bland indifference. So I spend the next couple of hours busily writing a spiteful piece about the staff of APCOA for my next column in a trade magazine, which gives me great pleasure but does little to cover my expenses for a wasted day! But we Heathrow regulars are eternal optimists; we always believe that tomorrow we'll have a blinding day!

In 1998 we were informed that we had to move to a new, custom-built site, because the present land we occupied near the entrance to the tunnel was prime real estate! BAA set up a site meeting and all the trade reps – myself included – were invited to offer their comments about what cabbies would like in the new feeder park. Unfortunately, like most other past BAA negotiations with our trade, the whole meeting was a complete sham and simply nothing more than a talking shop and a PR exercise. We found out later that the plans had already been approved by BAA management prior to our site meeting.

So we finally moved to our fully-computerised new site, complete with a new canteen, new toilets and two feeder parks with a total capacity of almost 500. But who would pay the extra costs for the brand-new computers, the extra traffic wardens needed and the extra cleaning staff to sweep the feeder parks? That's only meant to be a rhetorical question, because certainly BAA wasn't going to pay!

One would reasonably assume that any computer system in this day and age should be fully reliable and idiot proof! Not so, as proved by a small minority of devious London cabbies who would be quite capable of breaking out of Colditz – or even Alcatraz – if needs be! The taxi feeder park computer system at that time had one serious flaw and that was a human one! It was the duty of the traffic wardens who controlled all four terminal ranks to check badge numbers of all cabbies arriving on their terminal against their computer printouts and verify that all the drivers had gone through the system legally. No big deal there, that's what they were getting paid for. But human frailty being what it is, some wardens sloped off for a sly fag and a cuppa, while others, it was alleged, took a bung and turned a blind eye to the nefarious activities of the scallywags! Also, wardens stopped checking badge numbers against their computer printouts because of the row they were having with their bosses, the Met Police, for reducing the numbers of wardens on each rank from two to one. The wardens reckoned they couldn't check both numbers and printouts, so they decided to do neither and damn the outcome. So in one fell swoop the actions of some traffic wardens negated the tried and tested system and made the vastly expensive computer and its software completely useless. Now the honest cabbies at Heathrow were forced to reap the crooked crop sown by some lazy or, allegedly, dishonest wardens!

Then one bright day all the traffic wardens were returned to their normal duties at Heathrow and the taxi feeder park received a massive makeover with the installation of new barriers, new computers and a new private company to control the 'rabble'! These new state-of-the-art computers, coupled with personal tags for each and every cabbie, really DID work. Any cabbie could be tracked on the computer – wherever he went on the airport. So the practice of nicking a job from one of the terminals at will went out of the window overnight. The vast majority of honest cabbies were satisfied that the actions of the scallywags had been curtailed – but at what cost? All of this new computer equipment and the new private company running the show needed paying. And who would foot the bill – yet another rhetorical question?

5

HEATHROW IN THE 1990s

In the 1990s, before the new feeder park and its stringent policing, it was 'open-house' on the terminals and the devious cabbies were plucking a fair share of that crop. With the aid of mobile phones and mates down on the terminals, the wily cabbies would swoop like vultures when the call came that no badge numbers were being taken on a particular rank. It didn't bother them one iota that their mates in the feeder park were doing extra waiting time because of their actions. They only had one thought in their minds and that was attempting to nick as many fares in one day as humanly possible! Nothing changed for over two years – despite the fact that BAA were losing many thousands of pounds every week on the taxi entry charge. I wrote at the time that I doubted if anything would change until the wardens succeeded in their long-running dispute with their bosses.

In the absence of full-time supervision a small number of scallywags had perfected various scams such as covering up their computerised cab tags with silver paper so that it failed to register when they first entered the feeder park. Then, after waiting just a short while, they would follow the next group out and, after getting a 'go to control' on the exit reader, they'd go back to the warden's cabin to convince them that the entry reader was faulty and not recording some cabs. They were then issued with a ticket for the terminal of their choice and, bingo, they'd saved the cost of the entry fee and a possible two-hour wait!

Other rascals continually abused the radio ranks which should be used only by radio taxis waiting to pick up pre-booked fares. We worked long and hard for many months before BAA finally accepted our idea on a trial basis, so their future was tenuous to say the least! Yet the bad boys persisted in abusing them and in full view of their mates on the legal ranks. One has to pose the pertinent question: why? The answer is simple: the London Cabbie abides by their unwritten code of never 'shopping one of your own'. This is to be admired in many ways, but not when one of your own is blatantly stealing from their fellow drivers. Yet strange to relate, these scallywags stroll around the canteen admired by all – almost like modern-day Robin Hoods – but they certainly weren't robbing the rich!

Another not-quite-legal and often useful ploy was touting punters at the Airbus stops. At two quid a time it helped to pay for your diesel on your empty journey back to the airport – especially if you could chat up three or four punters in one hit. This practice became so rampant that the bus company reported the cabbies' activities to the 'Plod'. They in turn responded as though it was a major bank heist or a terrorist attack! Plain-clothes officers were despatched post-haste from Earls Court 'nick' to the Airbus stop in Cromwell Road where most of the punters were being purloined. But being the 'Plod', they sent the very same plain-clothes couple to the very same Airbus stop for a whole week, not bothering to reason that these cabbies might have some brains. One rainy day – and it really was falling down, one of the regulars pulled up at the Cromwell Road stop and he immediately recognised the two *agents provocateurs* looking rather soggy and sorry in the downpour. He leant out of his cab and beckoned the plain-clothes couple over. Their faces lit up in a beaming smile and they walked across, lovingly feeling their soggy warrants ready to be flashed. 'Do me a favour officer,' said the cabbie with a cheeky grin on his face. 'Could you tell me if my brake lights are both working properly?'

Another regular – who shall remain nameless – chatted up a foreign guy who was waiting at the same Airbus stop. The problem arose when he reached Heathrow and asked the foreign guy what terminal he wanted and was as sick as a parrot when the guy replied, 'De North Terminal.' The cabbie realised straight away that this guy had been waiting at the wrong bus-stop and wanted Gatwick Airport and, if he slung him out at Heathrow, he would soon be nicked. So, as we say in the cab trade, he 'wiped his mouth' and took the guy back to where he had first picked him up. After that shambles he decided to call it a day and went home!

I myself had a run in with the 'Plod' at the very same Airbus stop. I pulled up just before the stop so that the punters could see my board in the window that said, AIR BUS TAXI. Over came one of the 'Plod', flashed his warrant card and told me I would be reported for touting. 'But I haven't spoken to any punters, so how can I be touting?' I replied. He gave me a sickly grin then started quoting the law in a monotone voice as if I were some sort of dummy. 'Listen cabbie,' he said, 'Just having that sign in the window constitutes touting, plus the fact that you pulled up offering your services.' Reaching into my inside coat pocket I revealed my *pièce de résistance*, if you'll pardon my wording, and I handed him my official Airbus taxi licence. To say he was gobsmacked is an understatement! I had enough brains – as did about four other cabbies – to present myself at Charles House, Kensington High Street – not far from his nick – and fill in some forms to apply for an Airbus taxi licence. After some minimal payment I was officially licensed to pick up – but not to offer my services verbally – at ANY Airbus stop!

The poor old copper had completely lost the plot and walked away, mumbling that he'd never even heard of a bloody Airbus taxi licence. I shouted out in a friendly fashion, 'Be careful of the next two cabbies officer. I know Leon and 'Gorgeous' George are just behind me and they've both got official Airbus taxi licences as well!'

I recall writing an article in the trade press at the time strongly criticising the 'Plod' for their over-reaction and their wasting of valuable resources on such piddling offences. I also wrote that our trade should also make a formal complaint to the bus company about the touting activities of their OWN bus drivers. The bus contract stated that passengers should only be picked up and dropped off at official stops. However, for a sly 'back-hander' these drivers were picking up and dropping off willy-nilly – thus taking the potential fares away from cabbies! With the advent of time the ongoing problems were solved because the bus company went skint and the Airbus service was cancelled.

During the 1990s, and after half a century of the dog-eat-dog culture among the Heathrow regulars, plans started to be laid to form our own taxi-drivers' co-operative that would be called HALT (Heathrow Airport Licensed Taxis). The T&G and the LTDA reps banded together to form a committee and we convinced our own organisations that we weren't intending to take away their members, because this was a co-operative. The regulars at Heathrow have proved many times in the past that they are far more unified than the 'town drivers'. After voting in favour of a new co-operative, they then voted to raise money on the gate for a taxi desk in T1 because the touts were nicking so much of our work. As the co-operative grew and the numbers on the committee shrunk to a sensible working amount, the co-operative became more businesslike. Eventually, fully-manned taxi desks were installed in T2, T3 and T4. These taxi desks were manned in two shifts by experienced ex-taxi drivers who had lost their licences through ill-health. Every time the drivers bought a credit to enter the feeder park, a small sum was added on to pay part of the wages of the desk men.

By sheer hard graft and dedication, the HALT committee had got the four taxi desks into place, started a popular fixed-price voucher scheme and a credit card facility. In hindsight, this was a great concept in funding our own trade and should have put us way out of reach of the inevitable arrival of our opposition. It was a triumph and a great PR job for our trade and did a lot to convince BAA that cabbies could actually organise a business venture with some ability and success. As the now chairman of HALT, I noticed a decided change of attitude among the members of BAA's ground operations team when we met with them at monthly meetings. No longer was it a case of 'them and us'; they now treated us as business partners.

With the full support of all the regulars, our 'ship' should have now been well secure to repel any 'boarders'. But unfortunately in real life it doesn't happen like that. The HALT committee could have laid the ground rules better and I, as chairman for six years, must accept some of the blame. We were anticipating some three or four hundred members to join the new co-operative, so we set the quorum of 50 per cent at AGMs making sure that the AGMs weren't taken over by a 'rent-a-mob'. That anticipated three or four hundred turned into three or four THOUSAND, which meant we could never achieve a quorum! Obviously, the fact that our members could never elect a new committee – despite us exploring the legality of a rule-change – caused mounting dissention among many, and HALT gradually lost the support of the rank and file who had been with us from the beginning.

After some ten years away from the political arena at Heathrow I'm not up to date on the HALT issue. All I know is that I and many others worked our socks off for many long years to get the co-operative up and running. In between times I also set-up, obtained all the advertising, produced and edited the popular *HALT Magazine* for nearly six years, almost unaided. Why this popular magazine – which was a great advertisement for HALT and also self-supporting – was ever closed down I'll never know. The problem with success is that it also breeds envy and jealousy among certain individuals. Out of the blue this person – with the backing of a couple of his minions on the HALT executive – informed me that HE was closing down the popular magazine without any explanation why. That was a signal for me to pack my bags and resign my positions – and I haven't been back since!

But whatever happens in the future, nobody can ever take away those achievements from me.

6

THE HEATHROW REGULARS

I've always found the Heathrow regulars as nice enough people individually, but collectively they tend to become a bit aggressive and volatile. This probably stems from the fact that, way back in the past, all the 'town cabbies' resented their cartels and gangs and perceived them as a bunch of villains. Subsequently over the years, the airport regulars have become insular and tend to stick together and look after their own. However, their amazing generosity can never be questioned – it's legendary throughout the trade. The almost-daily collections they subscribe to for their sick mates and charities on the entry gate, is something else. Then there's the 'black book' going around the canteen on a daily basis, for yet another collection for a close mate who's very sick. Most of the guys and gals give a fiver or a tenner and sign their name in the book.

Way back in the 1990s, even the 'town cabbies' – who were always highly critical of the so-called 'airport villains' – would have the audacity to come out to Heathrow and apply for a 'list' (collection) for one of their mates – even though that particular individual may never have 'put on' in the feeder park. This loophole of abusing Heathrow cabbies' generosity was eventually plugged by making it a rule that any name on 'the list' had to have a Heathrow computer tag to accompany it!

What fascinates me is the fact that none of the many thousands of airport passengers have even an inkling of the existence of the massive taxi feeder park complex. They arrive at the terminals and see a dozen or more taxis on each rank and wrongly assume that this is the entire complement of taxis on the airport. They would be in for quite a shock if they went over to the Northern Perimeter Road and saw all the taxis lined up. Only then would they realise just how massive the Heathrow taxi operation is, with some 3,000 cab movements on a busy day and the two feeder parks – with a capacity of over 500 – filling and emptying four or five times over an 18-hour period. The cabbies' canteen, when full, is absolute bedlam because, and I know not why, most cabbies tend to shout when they talk, so all those operating their mobiles have to join in the shouting just to be heard! Speaking of the canteen, it would be remiss of me not to mention the guy who used to run it. Doug Sherry MBE was an absolute diamond geezer and worked his socks off for all the trade charities. Whenever one of the guys was looking for sponsorship in golf tournaments – or any other tournament come to that – the lovely Doug ALWAYS put his hand in his pocket. The last time I had the great pleasure of speaking to Doug he looked far from well and told me he was suffering from a long-term illness. Sadly, Doug passed away in May 2009.

Many of the hardcore regulars never work in town. Most of them go out to Heathrow empty to start work and wait their turn – sometimes as long as three hours. They do their 'ride' into town – or hopefully a long ride into the country – then turn around and come back again. It's certainly not about earning 'loads-a-money' by working this way all the time – the odds are they would probably earn more working in town. It's all about relaxing and the quality of life. They can enjoy a good meal in the canteen and a natter with their mates and, if they are feeling somewhat energetic, they can stand outside in the summer sunshine cleaning their cabs or even have a swim and a workout in the nearby gym. The bottom line is they don't have the hassle of enduring the daily traffic chaos in London for 8 hours a day.

There are many youngsters who now work Heathrow regularly – my son Nick included. However, by and large the majority of the regulars are made up of mature drivers who have been pushing a cab for thirty years or more and are suffering 'brain damage' from the many years of enduring the endless traffic chaos in London.

It has to be said though that there is another group of Heathrow 'regulars' whose antics upset the cabbies in town and even those at the airport. These are the 'mobile' cartels who bribe hotel porters into phoning them up when a 'cream' fare is ordered by a guest. They suddenly appear at a given hotel, take the 'cream' fare in full view of their fellow drivers sitting on the rank and blithely drive away. If this practice was confined to hotels without taxi ranks, then I would be the first to applaud it as good business acumen – but not with cabbies 'dying a death' on the ranks! In the old days a porter was looking for a half-a-crown 'drink' or so for 'services rendered'. In today's world of mounting inflation many of the mobile guys are paying out in excess of one quarter of the metered fare to Heathrow or one of the other London airports! These people seek to justify their nefarious practices by saying that if they didn't do it then all this 'cream' work would go to the minicabs. I personally don't buy that because I believe our trade is powerful enough to warn off the porters, via the management, or face a boycott of their hotel. The latest twist in this on-going saga is the rising price of the 'bung'. There are now an estimated 53,000 minicabs (or private hire vehicles) roaming the streets of London and the cabbies' old saying of, 'A fiver for a flyer', is now dead in the water! The opposition is upping the ante every week and the hotel porters are selecting the best offers without any sense of previous loyalties. And who do you think are screaming the loudest at this present escalating situation? I'll give you just one guess!

I suppose one could say that your 'certificate' of membership to the Heathrow 'regulars' club' is to be given a nickname. The guys out there are as sharp as a razor, with a wicked sense of humour. Just one faint hint of any physical impediment or peculiarity, no matter how small, and your nickname will follow you to your grave. It's fair to assume that since I departed from Heathrow, many of the guys with these following nicknames may have well gone to the 'big taxi rank in the sky'. They were all loveable rogues and their memory – and their nicknames – will live on.

First up: me. I smoke a pipe so I was Alf 'the Pipe' or, because of my regular articles in the trade press, it was sometimes 'Scoop'. We had 'Banana Nose' and 'Wing-Nuts' (who had prominent ears that stuck out a little). Then we had 'Flipper' (with the dodgy feet), 'Shuffler' (with the funny walk), Ted 'The Neck', Lenny 'Shoulders' and 'Karate' Larry. Other well-known regulars were Martin 'Rubber Lips' (or 'Rubber' as he was known), 'Laughing' John, 'Tannoy' (who was very noisy) and 'Trap One' (who never stopped talking). 'The Raging Bull' had a fearful temper and 'Mad' Barry, well, he was a bit mad and 'Gorgeous' George WAS gorgeous! Two brothers from north London were known as 'Sex and Violence' as one loved the ladies and the other loved whacking geezers!

And then we had 'Little Legs'. I need to tell this story about 'Little Legs' and whether it's true, or whether it's been expanded and exaggerated over the decades, I'm not too sure. The story goes that 'Little Legs' was waiting for the last flight in on T2, which was due to clear in about two hours' time. It was in the middle of winter and a freezing cold night. The cab on the point (front of the rank), pulled off with a 'walk up' job and all the other cabs moved up. But not 'Little Legs'; his battery had clapped out and nothing would make the engine fire, despite the boys giving him a jump start. The general opinion among the guys was an alternator or starter motor problem. So 'Little Legs' phoned his garage in the East End and told the night fitter he was on a good 'drink' if he could reach him before the last flight cleared. About an hour later the night fitter arrived driving an old un-plated cab, but even he couldn't get the old beast going. There was nothing left but to hook him up on the tow-chain. By this time the passengers were coming through off the last flight and, suddenly, 'Little Legs' was the only cab left on the rank. He spotted two guys, who turned out to be German, approaching the rank and he had a quick word with the night fitter to say nothing. As bold as brass, 'Little Legs' asked the punters their destination and when they replied, 'The Tower Thistle Hotel,' he put them into his cab and relayed their destination to the night fitter. So, as the story goes, off they went at a quiet and gentle pace, with 'Little Legs' chatting away to the Germans while they in turn, didn't appear the least perturbed! Amazingly they paid him off at the hotel without any comment and the night fitter got a sizeable 'drink' back at the garage. I can't help but picture the scene in the back of the cab, with one German saying to the other.

'These London taxis, Fritz, are very quiet don't you think?'

'Ja Hans, you are right, but I find them very slow and rather jerky!'

Highly improbable maybe, but a great story!

Many of the nicknames originated from where the guys lived, 'Bagshot' Bill, 'Ashford' 'Arry and 'Hounslow' Ted being examples. I recall many years ago 'Hounslow' Ted relating a very funny story to me. Ted, incidentally, packed up being a cabbie and went to work as a baggage handler on the airport many years back.

Ted was returning from a long job way out in the sticks and was heading down a country lane on his way back. He stopped at a level crossing, one of those that had a single barrier that came down. A moment later this old country boy with a huge dog in tow stopped on his left, closely followed by one of the country gents riding a horse. The big old dog didn't like the look of the horse and promptly pulled on his lead and barked at it causing the horse to shy up in the air, almost unseating its rider. Now the country gent on the horse has got the right needle and goes to whack the big old dog with his riding crop. Then all hell broke loose. The old country boy gives the rider some verbals and, tying the big old dog to the barrier, he rushes over to give the rider a dig. Suddenly the train whistled past and the barrier went up – as did the big old dog that was tied to it! Ted reckons they just managed to cut the big old dog down before it was strangled!

The nicknames 'Welsh' Bob, 'Scotch' John and 'Manchester' Ted are a clear indication of how far away many of these drivers lived. I was always fascinated at the vast distances some drivers travelled to reach Heathrow. Okay, so they obviously didn't go home every night; some stayed nearby with friends or relatives, while many of them would settle down in their cabs for the night, well wrapped up in their duvets. These guys were known as 'sleepers' and worked four 'long' shifts before heading home again. In my day, one of the best known of the 'sleepers' was 'Mr Pastry'. Legend has it that he used to cook his breakfast on a primus stove in the back of his cab!

My fascination with this subject of cabbies living far away lead me to try and discover just who lived the farthest distance from Heathrow. Towns along the south coast don't even rate in my top ten. Ditto for Somerset, Devon, Cornwall

– even Wales and Scotland! We are talking foreign climes here. Quite a few lived in Israel, France, Spain and Portugal and elsewhere on the Continent. I thought I'd discovered my winner when somebody tipped me off about 'Maltese' Arthur. Arthur does two months in London and the next two months or more in his elegant Maltese villa. Then I heard on the grapevine about the guy some call 'American' John, while others know him as 'Florida' John. He has got a pad in West Palm Beach, Florida, and does six months over here and six months over there. It must be a good saving on income tax! I thought I had finally found my all-time winner in Johnny 'Mack'. He lives, would you believe, in Thailand and travels over to London and Heathrow on a regular basis! However, that wasn't the end of my research because some friends of mine who run the Taxi Centre Repairs at the Royal Oak, Paddington, told me about a couple of their drivers who work three months a year. One is married to a Brazilian lady and comes over from Rio, while the other lives – wait for it – in Australia! Fascinating stuff, isn't it?

Where your parents originated from was another source for nicknames with Mick 'the Greek' and George 'the Greek', 'Italian' Tony and 'Italian' Vic being good examples. Your previous job immediately conjures up nicknames and the Heathrow regulars come from all walks of life. We've had ex-teachers and professors, former police inspectors, ex-professional footballers and boxers and a couple of well-known character actors. But it's those who did the menial jobs who get the long-lasting nicknames, such as Ron 'the Dust' (dustman), John 'the Fish', Danny 'the Docker', Sid 'the Grocer', 'Postman' Pat, Fred 'the Fireman', 'the Coalman' and 'Sheepdog' with his shaggy hair and beard!

One of the nicest guys around and someone who I played golf with many times was the late lamented 'Skipper' Dave. Now Dave got his nickname because he really WAS a 'Skipper', in fact he was a bomber pilot in the Second World

War. After many raids over Germany Dave was transferred to ferrying new bombers from Canada over the Atlantic to the UK. By the end of the war he was a Flight Lieutenant and finally reached the rank of Acting Squadron Leader, a really lovely man and sorely missed.

Maybe it could even be your regular mode of dress that created your nickname as in John 'The Hat', or 'Woolly Hat' George. Then we had this great character they called Fred 'The Suit'. Now Fred obviously got his nickname because he always – but always – wore a suit. But how he obtained his suits makes for a great story. Back in the 1970s and '80s most working-class families did their shopping with a home-delivered catalogue. You simply selected what you wanted, ordered it and paid on 'the weekly'. So Fred went over the top and ordered a very pricey suit and, on his way back from shopping some days later, he discovered a package on his front doorstep. It was in fact his pricey suit and the carrier had just dumped it there so he didn't have to redeliver the following day. 'Right,' thought Fred, 'this can be a little earner.' So after leaving it for a week or so, he phoned up the catalogue company and complained that he hadn't received his suit. They in turn informed him that it had been delivered on such-and-such a date. But Fred was adamant; he hadn't received the suit and he hadn't signed for anything! A week went by and Fred found yet another suit dumped on his doorstep. Again Fred left it for a couple of weeks, phoned up again and gave the catalogue company some right verbal, saying that he had waited over two months for his order and that he wasn't going to do business with the company ever again because they were incompetent! So now Fred had two very expensive suits that he hadn't paid a penny for. The scam was so easy he was tempted to use another catalogue company and get a different colour suit. So Fred adopted exactly the same procedure – with exactly the same carrier delivering the goods and dumping the parcel on his doorstep. And the same end product – two times over, or in this particular case, FOUR times over! Some may frown and say this is fraud, but hey, I'm not here to pass judgement, I'm only telling the story!

Back in those days anyone who had the slightest resemblance to TV actors – or even the characters in the TV ads – was given a nickname forever. We had a guy with glasses who was called 'the Milky Bar Kid'. Then there's 'Emmerdale', who is still an absolute pain because he's always 'hanging it up' at every West End hotel looking for clues. His latest ploy is 'hanging it up' at the set-down point at Paddington station – with a multitude of cabs waiting on the rank.

We had 'Brains' – as in *Thunderbirds* – 'the Muppet', 'Joe 90' and 'Emu'. Then we had 'Bilko', a dead ringer for Sergeant Bilko in the popular American sitcom of the 1960s. We even had 'The Jolly Green Giant'!

Perry 'Kettles' got his nickname because he loved repairing watches and 'Kettle' is cockney rhyming slang for 'Kettle and Hob', meaning the old fob watch. Even your driving warrants a nickname as exemplified by Chrissy 'Hot Wheels' and 'the Motorway Mouse'. Then there's the way you eat and your particular eating habits. 'Knives and Forks' is scoffing all the time, while 'Bread Roll Mick', obviously, has a bread roll with literally everything! 'Suffering' Peter is a lovely guy, but he gets his nickname because he can never back a winner, never wins at cards and always gets a 'wrong-un' (a bad job)!

Many of the Heathrow regulars enjoy a game of golf and I must tell this tale of one of the early-morning men Harold Fishman, also a regular golfing mate of mine. Harold went over for a holiday to visit his brother-in-law in Las Vegas and when the opportunity came up for a game on one of the many great courses, Harold jumped at the chance. But there was a slight problem; because it was Super Bowl Weekend, when they arrived at the course the whole area was packed out with gamblers to the casinos. The pro told them that there were six Texan guys waiting to tee-off and would they mind splitting up with them and making up two four-balls. 'No problem,' they said, and Harold introduced himself to the three Texans he was due to play with. He told me with a wry smile that they were all wearing big Stetsons and their golf bags were very expensive, really shiny leather jobs, with gold-plated tees! While waiting on the first tee one of the Texan guys came up to Harold and said, 'We normally play for five-a-hole, d' ya wanna join in the bet buddy?' Harold politely refused saying he was a bit rusty.

As luck would have it, Harold played like a champion and won about eight holes and, when he mentioned to his brother-in-law afterwards that he should have joined in the bet because he could have won about fifty dollars, his brother-in-law laughed, saying, 'You wouldn't have won eight holes if you realised that these guys were playing not for five dollars a hole, but FIVE Thousand Dollars a hole!' Harold went quite white when he heard that!

Another good golf mate of mine answers to the nickname of 'Back Nine'. This came about because he always made a total mess of the front nine, but played the back nine like a champ! His amusing tales follow.

For many years we trade reps – in tandem with the trade organisations – had been lobbying BAA to install a 'local ticket system'. We suggested at the time, that any driver on the rank should be allowed to return to any rank of his choice if he had a local journey and returned within thirty minutes. BAA eventually conceded to our persistent demands, but, like most other major organisations without a hands-on approach, they didn't have a clue on how to lay out the new ground rules and totally ignored our experienced input. So the local ticket system finally came into operation under the unfair rules of BAA. Drivers would only be allowed to return to the ranks if they had a fare to any of the local hotels, regardless of if the address asked for was adjacent to that particular hotel. This was obviously a recipe for playing the high game and, in effect, totally unfair on some unfortunate cabbies.

My old golf mate 'Back Nine' was sitting on the point of Terminal 2 when up strolled a guy who was probably German. He asks 'Back Nine' to take him to an address in the Bath Road – just outside the airport. 'Back Nine' has a quick look to see where the lady traffic warden is and says to the German guy, 'When the traffic warden asks you where you're going, tell her the Post House hotel. Do you understand?' The German guy stood there for a minute, then a smile crossed his face just as if he knew what the scam was all about. 'Ja, ja,' he replied, still smiling away, 'I understand what you are telling me.' When the lady traffic warden came up to 'Back Nine's' cab he asked her for a return ticket to the Post House hotel. And, like most other traffic wardens at Heathrow (who never believed the cabbies), she checked it out by opening the rear door and asking the passenger his destination. The German guy, still smiling at being involved in this subterfuge replied. 'I go to number so-and-so, the Bath Road, but first the driver wants to go to the post office.' Exit 'Back Nine' with egg on his face and with another two-hour-wait to look forward to after a four quid fare!

'Back Nine' had another calamity recently when he was working in town. He got a fare from Russell Square to Brixton Hill and, as he pulled away, another hand went up. Because it was very busy that night, he asked the passenger if he would mind sharing if the guy was going in the same direction – for a special discount of course – and the punter said it was no problem. The other customer turned out to be Irish and was going to Streatham – just past Brixton Hill – so 'Back Nine' again got the nod when he asked him if he minded sharing.

Anyway, he dropped the first punter off and knocked a couple of quid off the fare, but when Paddy jumped out at Streatham he just walked away with a, 'Thank you very much, sir.' So 'Back Nine' went after him and asked about the fare. 'Oh, I haven't got any money, sir,' said Paddy. 'I was just hitching a lift when you stopped and asked me if I wanted to share your car!' Exit 'Back Nine' with more egg on his face!

Way back in the 'bad old days' the relationship between the cabbies and the Heathrow police was at an all-time low. We resented their authoritarian manner, while they considered us just 'bolshy' cabbies. Then an unpleasant incident occurred that was to inflame the cabbies and break down any possible reconciliation between the two factions for many years to come. I was so incensed by the reprehensible position that the police had adopted that I wrote a scathing article about it in a trade magazine and entitled it, 'Airport Crime Rate Slashed as Police Nab Notorious Omelette and Chips Gang'. This is the article, with just some names omitted:

> Those hairy custodians of the law at London's Heathrow Airport, who devote much of their duty hours playing at being parking attendants and cat-and-mouse with that quaint, rare and elusive 'Green-Badger', have once again firmly stuck their size-fourteen beetle-crushers into, what seemingly appeared a pot of gold, and come out with a sock full of horse manure! They have extended their personal vendetta against all cabmen to the realms of unbelievable farce and had them rolling in the aisles in the taxi feeder park. It's true the gold bullion is still disappearing at regular intervals, as are many diamond shipments. Pilfering is rife and thousands of pounds worth of goodies are spirited away every week – not forgetting all the spirits. Drug smuggling is on the increase,

while pickpockets and unlicensed touts roam the terminals almost at will, yet still the 'Bluebottles' relentlessly pursue the 'Green-Badger'. And now, they wrongly believe, at long last, they have success. Totally oblivious to the organised gangs systematically helping themselves to all the many goodies at 'Thief-Row', the lumbering airport 'Bluebottles' (who are specially hand-picked from the thickest in their class) have stuttered into action by swooping on the 'Omelette and Chips Gang', automatically guaranteeing the force at least four lines on the back page of *The Berks and Bucks Examiner* – plus of course a policy of sullen, non-cooperation from cabmen for many years to come.

These are the true facts of this ridiculous case. Ever since the airport canteen was closed for refurbishment, it has been common practice among the regulars to borrow a staff meal card from one of the airport employees and go and get some grub at a reasonable price. How many of us have 'bent' the law at one time or another by borrowing a trade card for the Houndsditch Warehouse, or some other trade-card store? I know it is technically illegal, but if there's no canteen for cabmen and, they are at the airport all day supplying a service, then why shouldn't they be allowed to use the staff canteen to get a meal at subsidised rates? The offence might warrant a diplomatic, ''Op it cabbie or I'll nick you,' or even a warning notice stuck up in the feeder park, but does it really necessitate such serious charges as 'obtaining goods by deception', 'handling stolen property' – that's if you refuse to reveal who you borrowed the card from – or 'obtaining pecuniary advantage'? And does it really necessitate a shocking squandering of rate payers' money and a complete waste of the already-overworked legal system when this piddling offence is remanded month after month, until finally being settled, grossly unfairly to my mind, at Reading Crown Court?

One of my old golf mates who has worked the airport for the past ten years without ever having been nicked (which in itself is something of an achievement), was quietly eating his omelette and chips in the staff canteen some fourteen months ago when his nightmare began. And, after fourteen months of worry – with his wife on the point of a nervous breakdown – incompetent legal aid that was costing him even more money and with the police changing the charges more frequently than

> they changed their socks, his nightmare came to a merciful end recently at Reading Crown Court. The judge interpreted the guilty verdict as an excuse to dispense a bit of eighteenth-century law against this 'wretched-fellow'. His Honour felt fit to crucify this family man for daring to save about 50p on his meal by fining him a staggering £425, which was only a £100 fine but with £325 costs! Yet in the same court in the same week, a rapist was bound over with a smaller fine! So, according to the morals of English Law, it's cheaper to have an illegal bit on the side than it is to eat omelette and chips in the staff canteen at Heathrow with a borrowed meal card?
>
> The trouble is, with cases like this, it doesn't end there for the licensed cabbie. When the papers reach the Public Carriage Office, some of the 'brain dead' up there will just look at the verdict and not the pettiness these charges appertain to. So please don't consider revoking his licence for such a petty offence blown out of all proportion. The guy has been punished more than enough, so please give us a sign that we are not being manipulated by morons!

Our poor relations with the Ol' Bill were further exacerbated when one of their 'planks' posted a notice on the door of our canteen. It read something like this. 'All taxi-drivers are hereby warned that buying stolen goods from strangers is a criminal offence and will be dealt with as such.' Okay, so there were some shady characters creeping around the feeder park flogging cheap razors, copies of A–Zs and batteries. But come on, what licensed driver in his right mind would want to risk jeopardising his living by buying crappy, hooky gear? Most of us were disgusted at this affront, because we reckoned it branded us all as potential criminals. Then one of the guys wrote in bold letters at the bottom of the notice, 'There are more coppers in jail than cab drivers!' The notice was swiftly removed and never reappeared!

I believe nowadays that the relationship between the cabbies and the airport police is not as bad as it used to be. Even so, Mick, a mate of mine, had a bad experience with them recently. Like any good cabbie worth his salt he was helping an old couple into T3 with their trolleys, but when he returned he discovered somebody had nicked his moneybag. There wasn't a lot of dough in it, just some loose change, but it did contain his cab licence. So he promptly headed for the police station to report the theft. The WPC on the computer wasn't exactly helpful, especially when my mate said, 'If you switch on the CCTV cameras that show the taxi rank at T3, you'll see the person who nicked my bag.' She sniffed loudly and, looking at my mate as though he was something stuck on the bottom of her shoe, she said icily, 'We can't switch on the CCTV cameras because it's not a high-profile crime!'

So that was that and Mick walked out in a huff. There was a happy ending to this story despite the intransigence of the police. About a month later my mate received his cab licence in the post. Either some good Samaritan had found it and posted it on or – and this is a big 'or' – the thief had been stricken with a guilty conscience and posted it; I think not!

Another recent incident goes to show that the Heathrow police still don't go a lot on liking taxi drivers. Two of the well-known regulars were having a bit of exercise by walking around in the vicinity of the taxi feeder park and happened to pass a full skip. They couldn't help but notice some computer equipment sticking out of the top, so in they jumped to salvage a couple of computer screens in seemingly good nick – no pun intended! They reckoned all this had been thrown out by somebody and, as junk, they were perfectly entitled to take it away. Not so, said the Ol' Bill, who had suddenly arrived on the scene as though it was some sort of terrorist threat. They informed the two cabbies that the contents of the skip were the property of the skip owner. They were accused of theft and banged up in the Heathrow 'nick' for THREE long hours, until common sense prevailed and they were released.

I am told they still can't drive past a skip without having a peek inside!

7

SOME SAD – BUT MANY AMUSING – FARES FROM HEATHROW

Those cabbies who work at Heathrow regularly learn to be very philosophical in their outlook on life. The person or persons who approach their cab – especially at night – are on the whole just respectable business people wanting to get home. But – and here's where many years of experience comes into play – you have to learn to spot a 'wrong-un' and not be tempted into taking risks simply because it's a long fare and worth big bucks! If your sixth-sense is roused and the hairs on the nape of your neck start to stiffen, just say 'no thank you'. How are you to know that maybe this pleasant gentleman wanting to go to 'High Street China' isn't a serial killer or a weirdo?

I recall many years ago being the second cab on the Paddington rank one Sunday afternoon and a couple of guys, looking slightly bedraggled, came up to the first cab and asked to go to Epping. He refused politely (as he is legally entitled to do because the fare was over 6 miles) and I also refused because the hairs on the back of my neck were feeling strange. The guy with the third cab accepted the fare gratefully because he lived near Epping. Sadly, he never saw his home again; the police found him dead in Epping Forest, shot in the back of the head by the two guys who were escaped convicts.

It's all very well some of you reading this saying in a dismissive fashion, 'What a load of absolute codswallop, is this guy for real?' However, I suggest you wouldn't be saying that if you felt a knife being stuck into the back of your neck in some quiet country lane. This is exactly what happened to a cabbie who was a neighbour of mine in north London. 'Hampstead' Bryon was a lovely gentle guy and enjoyed nothing better than playing kalooki with his mates in the airport canteen. He thought his luck was in when a guy came up to the rank and asked how much to Leeds in Yorkshire. Bryon negotiated a fair price and off they went. By the time they reached Leeds, it was dark and very deserted where the guy asked him to pull up. Without warning the guy suddenly put his arm through the open partition window and stabbed Bryon in the back of the neck with a knife. He ran off and was never caught and brought to justice. Thankfully Bryon recovered from this cowardly attack, but sadly, not too-many-years later, he died suddenly. Now I'm not privy to Bryon's medical history, but if he did have a dodgy ticker, then the shocking trauma he had suffered may well have contributed to his premature death.

Another story – this time a humorous one – concerns this cabbie who took a 'bowler-hat' (a City gent) to Ipswich. Maybe I've got a weird sense of humour, but I find this story hilarious. The guy was quite chatty all the way up to Ipswich, telling the driver he lives in a home in the country and that he's going up to visit his old mum who lives alone. The cabbie didn't think twice when his passenger said 'he lived in a home in the country' and not 'a house', but the first hint of doubt came into his head when he was directed into a slightly scruffy housing estate on the edge of town. The nagging doubts multiplied when he was asked to stop outside an equally scruffy old cottage and a little, grey-haired old lady came running out and up to the cab shouting in an angry voice, 'Robert, you're a very naughty boy! I told you never to do this again!' The cabbie's eyes almost popped out of his head when the once-assured and cocky 'bowler hat' suddenly burst into tears saying, 'I'm sorry mummy but I couldn't wait to see you.' Now, as they say in our trade, the cabbie's 'bottle' had gone and he realised he could be up the creek without the proverbial paddle. Taking a deep breath the cabbie approached the little old lady and said laconically – almost as if he hadn't heard a thing that had been going on – 'I don't know what it's all about, luv, and, quite honestly, I don't want to know 'cos it's none of my business. All I want is my money and I'll be on my way.' The little old lady looked at the cabbie with some pity in her eyes and replied in a matter of fact tone, 'Oh, I'm sorry driver you're not going to get any money. My son lives in a mental home and has done this a couple of times before – despite previous scoldings. As with the other drivers you are perfectly entitled to go to the police and report it, but I'm afraid you'll get the same answer they did. Sadly my son is certified so as such he is not responsible for his actions – and neither am I.'

To say the cabbie was gob-smacked would be an understatement, but he only had to look at the now-whimpering 'bowler-hat' to realise he was an out and out nutcase! So what to do now, he thought to himself? Shall I go down the local nick and try my luck, or shall I call the Ol' Bill and get them to come over, even though it looks dead in the water? He pondered his options as he pulled away, giving the nutcase a mouthful of expletives on the way! Calling the Ol' Bill out on an obvious wasted journey would take hours, so the cabbie decided to cut his losses and head for the A12 and London. With the benefit of hindsight, this seems a classic example of a cabbie charging in blindly to a very long fare without first checking out some simple facts. Was the passenger paying with cash or a credit card, if it was cash, would he mind putting some up front as a goodwill gesture? Was there anything about this guy that didn't seem right and, did the cabbie get that feeling in the hairs on the nape of his neck? Always worth checking . . .

By and large the Heathrow regulars are basically honest – as are the London cabbies and, come to that, so are most other cabbies. But, when it comes to buying some 'hooky gear' that's maybe 'fallen off the back of a lorry', at a knock-down price, well that's a different story! For obvious reasons I can't say the name of this Heathrow regular, but he happened to be Irish, so we'll call him 'Paddy'. Anyway, Paddy met a contact in town one evening and purchased a length of very expensive mohair cloth that his mate, a tailor, would make into a blinding suit. He put it into the luggage compartment in his cab and made his way home. As often happens, when you want a copper, you can never find one. But when you DON'T want one, they appear from all over the place and Paddy drove straight into a police road block. He was asked the same sort of police questions like, 'where are you heading for driver?' and, 'have you been working and boozing?' But they seemed satisfied with his replies until one of them, spotting the cloth in the luggage compartment, said, 'What's that you've got in there cabbie?' Now Paddy had to think very quickly and answer very assuredly.

'Well now,' he said, 'For sure, that there cloth was left in my taxi by my last fare and I'm just on my way to drop it into 'so-and-so' police station.' The two coppers look at each other with a knowing smirk on their faces – well aware that Paddy was 'at it' – but they had to take his word.

'Right cabbie,' said one of the coppers, 'this is what's going to happen. I'm going to check out 'so-and so' nick later – just to make sure you've dropped the stuff off – okay? Now, on your way mate – and don't forget your last delivery!'

1. It's muddy out there! Heathrow's first terminal as it appeared in 1946.

. Not bad for a tent. The interior of Heathrow's terminal in 1946.

3 & 4. People from all over the world and from all walks of life do the Knowledge.

5. The All Nations Taxi Shelter. This shelter was named after the Great Exhibition of 1851.

6. An LTDA boycott of one of London's major hotels. The placards say it all.

7. Chris Harrison, HALT's treasurer in the 1990s.

. Hard at work in the HALT office.

9. Waiting on the terminal rank at Terminal 2, where the European flights land.

10. The rank on Terminal 5.

11. The taxi feeder rank on the massive new construction that is Terminal 5.

12. Loading up on Terminal 2.

3. Just two cabs waiting on Terminal 2 – it won't be long before I'm on my way.

14. On the terminal ranks, waiting for the long-haul arrivals at Terminal 3.

15. Still more waiting outside Terminal 3's arrivals.

16. HALT committee posing on our stand marking the fiftieth anniversary of Heathrow.

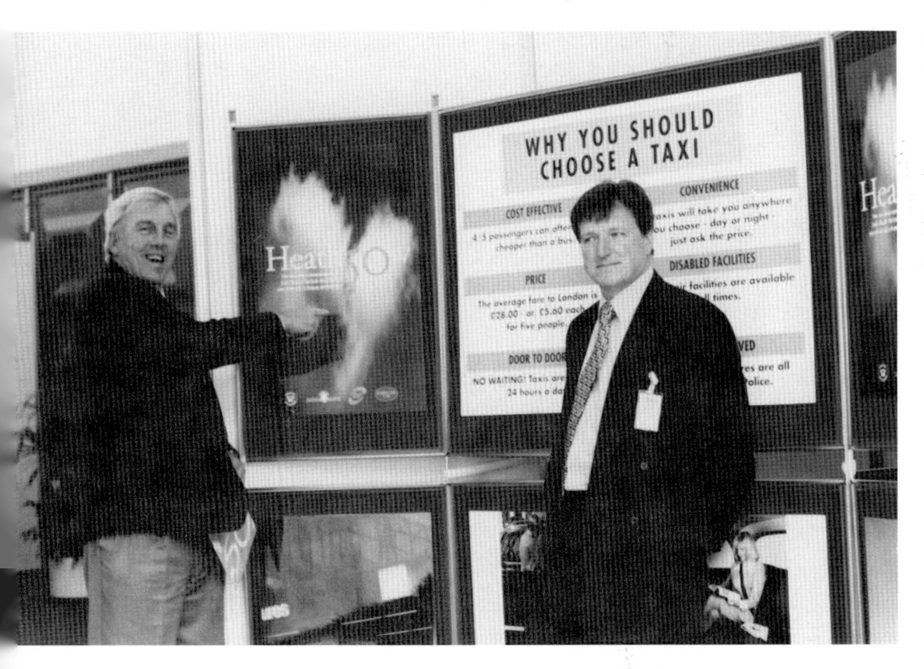

17. Posing with Colin Evans at HALT's stand at Heathrow's fiftieth anniversary.

18. Concorde and the Red Arrows fly past, celebrating the fiftieth anniversary of Heathrow.

19. *Opposite, bottom:* Her Majesty arrives on the fiftieth anniversary.

20. *Below:* The royal couple study plans for the future.

21. Bill Morris, the former boss of the TGWU and me. How times have changed in a decade because now Bill, a very likeable guy, has been elevated to the peerage and is now Lord Morris of Handsworth.

22. The entry barrier to the feeder park.

23. Entering the taxi feeder park.

24. With over 180,000 passengers passing through Heathrow each day, it's no wonder so many taxis are needed.

25. Blossom time in the taxi feeder park.

26. Collecting at the gate for a sick mate.

27. 'Sergeant Bilko' flogging his wares.

28. Watch out, the PCO's about, so keep those cabs nice and shiny!

29. Another long wait. Shall I go to the gym for a workout, have a game of cards in the canteen or just have a kip?

30. All nice and shiny in the airport canteen.

31. Anyone for bangers?

32. Time to eat in the Heathrow canteen.

33. A half-empty canteen – it must be early morning.

34. You can't beat a game of cards to while away the time.

35. My mate and fellow author Mick Rose.

36. Ellis the cool dude in the LTDA office.

37. The planes land just a stone's throw from the taxi feeder park.

38. Taxis and jumbo jets rubbing shoulders.

However, Paddy wasn't too bothered after he checked the cloth in at the nick. He knew it was 'hooky' and that nobody would claim it. And he knew full well that after three months the Lost Property Office, once situated in the same building as the Public Carriage Office, would ring him up and ask him to come in and claim it. Then a strange thing happened about a month later. He got an official form from the LPO informing him that the cloth had been claimed by its 'rightful owner'. Now Paddy was in a whirlpool of indecision. If he accused the Ol' Bill of nicking his cloth, then he could have lost his cab licence if it went pear-shaped. On the other hand, if he admitted the cloth was is fact 'hooky gear', then again he could lose his cab licence. So, as we say in the trade, he 'wiped his mouth' and said nowt!

Talking of the Lost Property Office brings back some fond memories for me. For many years the LPO was an integral part of all London cabbies' lives, whether they worked at Heathrow or in town. Any item found in the back of a London taxi had to be handed in at a police station of your choice within twenty-four hours. In the old days, ten little grey vans went out every weeknight to collect lost property from EVERY single police station in the Metropolitan Police District (the LPO was closed Saturdays and Sundays). That meant ALL lost property could be at the LPO ready for claiming within twenty-four hours. Their system seemed to work, because back in 1975 there were 9,538 items handed in and 3,895 were restored to their 'rightful owners' (that's around 43 per cent) and 2,146 were returned to cabbies. So when my editor on the trade magazine asked me to write a major feature on the LPO, I couldn't wait for my all-day visit. It was a fascinating experience – especially when visiting the heavily bolted room known to the staff as 'the safe' but looking more like Aladdin's Cave. This was where they stored all the valuable Class One property. There were shelves packed full with expensive cameras that must have been worth many thousands of pounds. I managed to get a peek into some of the boxes packed with jewellery. How some of these wealthy ladies and celebrities could possibly leave such priceless necklaces and rings in the backs of taxis, I don't know! Were they under the influence of something?

Beneath all the pretty and expensive items were all the 'nasties' – a frightening collection of daggers, flick-knives and wicked-looking swordsticks. Fancy having something like that stuck in the back of your neck one dark night on Clapham Common? I wouldn't think the owners of these weapons would have the audacity to claim them!

Next stop was the storeroom for the less valuable Class Two category property. Here again, was shelf after shelf full of holdalls, gloves, shoes, suitcases and just about any other conceivable item you could think of. How on earth can somebody leave a push-chair or a coffee table in the back of a cab? And what about the men's shoes on display; did they take them off in the cab and walk home in their socks?

The most valuable item ever handed in was a wallet containing over £20,000 worth of uncut diamonds – I bet the delivery boy got a roasting when he went back to Hatton Garden to tell his boss! The heaviest was an industrial coffee urn about 3ft in height! The most unusual and bulkiest, a complete disco with two amplifiers and 700 records, needed three coppers to unload it! It appeared that the cabbie with the load was instructed by the DJ to follow his car, but lost him, so he handed in the gear. The DJ came screaming into the LPO the following day accusing cabbies of being 'tea-leaves' (thieves).

Some forgetful person also left a map of the USA Greyhound bus routes. Nothing too unusual about that, you may be saying, but it was in a frame measuring 5ft long and 4ft high! I did hear a story making the rounds in the trade at that time of a cabbie handing in a pushchair – with a baby still sitting in it! The LPO moved to Baker Street some years later.

John, an airport mate once phoned me and said that the Arabs he had taken into a posh West End hotel had left a large, fat wallet in his cab. I was intrigued. He told me it contained about £4,000 and asked me for some advice; should he take a chance and keep it, or should he hand it in? I warned him he was taking a chance of losing his cab licence if he decided to keep it, because it would be relatively easy for him to be traced via his group number and the time he left the feeder park – plus the fact that the Arabs would be shown mug-shots of every licensed driver. Anyway John phoned me some time later and said he HAD handed in the wallet and that the 'barrack-room lawyers' in the cab shelter told him he would be on a 10 per cent reward, which would be around £400. He assumed they were correct and had booked a luxury weekend in Paris for himself and his wife. Now after my day at the LPO I had discovered that they utilised a diminishing scale of reward, so I told him to hold his horses while I checked my sums. After checking my sums I replied, 'I'm sorry John boy, but I've worked it out on the diminishing scale that you only stand to get £29.50p. So you'll have to settle for a dirty weekend in Southend!' He phoned me a while later to tell me I had got my sums wrong, he had in fact got thirty quid!

For the benefit of my cabbie readers in London, this is the diminishing scale of reward as utilised by the LPO in those days: 15 per cent up to £10 value, 10 per cent of £20 value, 7.5 per cent to £50 value, 5 per cent £50 to £200 value, 2.5 per cent £200 to £500 value. Anything valued over £500 gave just 1 per cent. Some people tend to moan at the low rate of reward, but think about it: if you found any lost property on London transport, you would get absolutely nothing as a reward. That still doesn't mean that anything you find on a bus or tube should be thrown into the back of a cab!

While on the subject of Arabs, I must relate the hilarious story told by the late 'Big Siddy' Foreman. He took three

Arabs from Heathrow to the very posh Brown's Hotel in Mayfair. One of the Arabs spoke excellent English and was obviously the 'boss-man'. Back in those far-off days they were doing major building works next to the hotel and so naturally, there were piles of sand all over the place. Anyway while the 'boss-man' was paying off 'Siddy', the two other Arabs wandered over to the sand, lifted up their white robes and proceeded to squat down and do their business! 'Big Siddy' couldn't help but gawp at these goings-on, with his eyes wide in utter disbelief. But the 'boss-man' Arab just said casually, 'Oh, that's normal for them, they are two of my workers and they live way out in the desert!'

Another one of the regular nightmen at Heathrow, who was a champion professional boxer in his younger days (and had a wicked temper), picked up this posh geezer on T2 and was asked the price of the fare to deepest Berkshire. The guy screamed the place down when he was told how much, but still got into the cab moaning like mad and never stopped moaning all the way to the end of the journey. By the time they arrived the rain was lashing down and our man was directed through the gates of a huge manor house. He drove up a circular drive and past a lush green lawn that looked as though it had been finely cut with a pair of scissors. The posh geezer jumped out, thrust the exact money into the cabbie's hand and said, 'I will be reporting you for gross overcharging and ripping off the public.' He then stormed up the massive steps and slammed the door! Now our man is fuming; the fare was outside the Metropolitan Police District and he hadn't ripped him off because that was the price on the list approved by BAA. So, in his anger, he did a sharp right turn and drove straight across the manicured lawn!

If you're a London cabbie, incidents like this can happen all the time. In fact if I were to write a sitcom about all the weird and wonderful happenings that I've heard over my many years of driving, the producer would probably knock it back as being unrealistic. Take the case of another Heathrow regular, who was lucky enough to pick up an airport fare at one of the West End hotels. The porter started loading up three huge cabin trunks in the back of his cab and they were so large they needed to be standing upright. So off our man went, realising that he needed to fill up with some diesel before reaching the M4. The favourite filling-up point for the guys and gals who work Heathrow is the service station just over the Hammersmith flyover. So our man stops the meter, jumps out and informs the guy that he won't be a minute. He returns after paying for his diesel and continues on his way, telling the passenger he can soon make up for the time lost in the filling station. They arrive at Heathrow and our man says, 'That was very quick sir, wasn't it?' He then starts to unload the huge cabin trunks. After emptying the cab, he suddenly realises his passenger is not in there, but maybe he got out via the offside door, he thinks to himself. But no, there's not a sign of him anywhere. Now our man is getting a little concerned thinking maybe his fare threw himself onto the M4 while he was doing 70mph! So he called the Ol' Bill over to help him solve the mystery. They searched the cab, both back and front and, being the Ol' Bill, they even looked underneath the cab, but still no sign of the missing punter. The mystery of the missing punter was finally solved when another cab, with a loud blast of the horn, pulled up alongside and out jumped the red-faced punter. He had made a call of nature and was emptying out while our man was filling up. The moral of this story is, don't slope off for a quick pee without first informing your cabbie, because it could well cost you 'double-bubble'!

Still on the same theme, a young cabbie was on the T4 rank late one evening when his job came out – a little old lady who only wanted to go to the Master Robert Hotel on the A4. Okay, so it was getting late and he would have probably 'blown out' (been too late for another fare) when he returned, so he went into one and kicked up a terrible fuss, making the dear old lady very embarrassed. He stormed down to the traffic warden to get his return ticket then stormed back into his cab, jumped in and set off on a 'white-knuckle' ride down the A4. Screeching onto the forecourt he jumped out to get rid of the old lady as soon as possible and was so, so surprised to find there was nobody in the back. The dear old lady, having been totally embarrassed by this cretin, had disappeared back into the terminal while the driver went to get his return ticket. I'm happy to report that he did in fact 'blow out' as well!

A very dear friend of mine who has worked Heathrow for many years told me about his funny story a long time ago. He was heading down Finchley Road on his way into town and hailed by a little old lady carrying a battered old case. She asked for Winchester, so he naturally assumed she meant Winchester Road, just around the corner in Swiss Cottage. That will suit me fine he thought, drop her off and stick it on the rank at the once-named Holiday Inn Swiss Cottage and maybe stand half a chance of getting off to the airport. But when he pulled up in Winchester Road, the old girl said, 'No dearie, not here. I want Winchester in Hampshire!' Now my friend is slightly nonplussed to say the least and told the old girl that going to Winchester will cost her well over one hundred pounds. 'That's no problem dearie,' she replied, 'my son has got a big estate in Winchester. He told me to get a taxi and he's going to pay the fare.' Now this is when your experience and perception comes into its own. The little old lady was perfectly lucid and had all her marbles. In fact she could have been his mum or anyone else's mum, so, he took a chance and started heading for Winchester.

A couple of hours later he was directed up a country lane on the outskirts of Winchester and told to turn left through some iron gates. He felt much more assured as he drove up a long and elegant drive and stopped outside a large manor house. His relief was complete when a guy came out of the manor house, dressed like a country gent in tweeds and rushed over to his cab. He was obviously the wealthy son and he gave his mum a big hug before coming up to my mate enquiring how much. My mate replied with a big grin on his face, 'That's exactly one hundred and forty pounds, sir' – that in itself tells you how old this story is! Well my mate thought the country gent was going to faint as he spluttered, with an incredulous look on his face, 'One hundred and forty pounds from Winchester station, that's ridiculous!' Then, suddenly, the awful realisation came over him and turning to his old mum he said curtly, 'Mummy, when I phoned you I told you to get a train from Waterloo to Winchester and then a taxi to here. Did you hire this taxi in London?' The little old lady just nodded benignly and walked off into the big house, totally oblivious of her mistake. Now the country gent is desperately searching through his pockets for some readies and manages to rustle up a hundred quid. He calls out a couple of his servants and the gardener and they manage to club together and make up forty quid in pound coins and silver! My mate said a big thank you and headed for Heathrow with a big grin on his face!

The guys and gals who work Heathrow on a regular basis are normally always on the ball when often confronted with foreign folk who can't speak English and haven't got a clue where they are going. Nevertheless, there have been numerous occasions when Brentford in Middlesex has been confused with Brentwood in Essex – some 30 miles further on. Even Milton Keynes was once called Maidstone, Kent, by one foreign guy. The cabbie, who believe it or not actually lived a stone's throw from Milton Keyes, was lumbered with a tour of Kent before finally reaching home! I came unstuck on one occasion when I was so eager not to lose a 'roader' that I priced a fare to Bagshot in Berkshire, instead of it being Didcot in Oxfordshire – again a difference of over 30 miles.

Once, one of the guys on the rank in front of me said there was a foreign chap wanting to go to Mornington Crescent and, knowing I lived in Camden Town, asked me if I'd like the job? I was chuffed. It was only when we were half way down the M4 and the guy tapped on the window that I realised something wasn't quite right. I pulled on to the hard shoulder and the guy explained in broken English that he had been told this address was very near the airport. So, a closer scrutiny of the address on the letter he showed me and the awful truth dawned on me; he wanted Mornington Crescent, Cranford, which is just outside the airport on the Bath Road! So I took the next turn off on the motorway and headed back from whence I came and we compromised when it came to the cost of the fare!

Yet another mix-up with the proper destination happened one Saturday morning on Terminal 2. The guy on point was trying desperately to get a fare into central London so he could go and see his favourite football team, Millwall, play at The Den. When a Swedish couple asked to go to the Hampton Court Palace Hotel, the guy was gutted. So he asked the cab behind if he would do him a favour and take the job. Now this second cab was an old golf mate of mine who was nicknamed 'Adolf', after you-know-who, because when he played golf he hated bunkers! So 'Adolf' said he would help the guy out and loaded up the passengers. Before leaving he asked some of the guys exactly the whereabouts of this hotel in Hampton Court. Their info was conflicting to say the least, with some saying 'turn right over Hampton Court Bridge,' while others were saying, 'turn left over the bridge.' Our man decided to take a chance with the fare and to ask one of the locals when he arrived at the destination. This turned out to be a not-very-good idea because nobody had a clue to its whereabouts and, after doing the guided tour of Hampton Court, 'Adolf' asked the Swedish couple if they had an address for the hotel. Indeed they had because they had pre-booked it on the internet. This is the punch-line. The grand-sounding Hampton Court Palace Hotel was actually some 20 miles away from King Henry VIII's world-famous palace at Hampton Court. It was actually situated in Hampton Street, a seedy and not-very-salubrious south London backstreet – just behind the Elephant & Castle. And, I might add, just fifteen minutes away from the first cab-driver's favourite football club! So 'Adolf's' kindness was handsomely rewarded with a sizeable fare and, to paraphrase this old saying that I think ticks all the boxes, 'Being kind to others can bring kindness to you!'

This next old chestnut is about a Yank with the deep Southern drawl who asked one of the guys to take him to what sounded like Tooting Common. When they arrived, he asked the driver where the exhibition was and the driver naturally replied, 'Wot bloody exhibition?' Then the penny finally dropped; he wanted the Tutankhamun exibition at the British Museum. Say 'Tut's' name in an American accent and you will know why! Don't forget guys and gals, ALWAYS check the destination before you leave because it could well save you a lot of aggro!

One of my mates who works at Heathrow regularly, e-mailed me recently. Mick Rose is a fellow trade journalist and author and told me about an amusing incident that had occurred to him recently. He was hanging about on T3 waiting for a fare when a little Italian guy came up to him and said, 'I want-a eight-a taxis.' Now Mick thinks this is some sort of wind up from a nutcase and replies somewhat sarcastically, 'You must be wanting to move about forty people mate!' Imagine his surprise when the little Italian guy says, 'Si, si, we have forty people to put into eight-a taxis and we go to St Albans.' Now Mick is seriously interested because a ride to St Albans is big bucks, so he went back to the next seven cabs on the rank and got the nod after he had agreed a fair price. It turned out that these guys were a top-flight Italian football team who were due to play Arsenal the following day and their coach had been stopped by the airport police for having bald tyres. So Mick loaded them all up and they all followed him in convoy to the very plush Sopwell House Hotel in St Albans. Mick told me he was slightly nervous when he went to see the hotel manager for the dough, but she didn't bat an eyelid when she counted about over £700 in readies!

While on the subject of St Albans, another one of the regulars was making his way home up the Barnet Way after a not-very-good day. He noticed the traffic building up in front and slowed down because part of the nearside carriageway had been coned off for road works. As he drove slowly past, the massive digger on site suddenly and for no apparent reason swung round and the wicked steel jaws ripped open the nearside of his cab. The impact was so severe that the central pillar was chopped in half which caused the roof to collapse on the unfortunate cabbie and he was trapped inside. Our man was eventually cut out of the cab by firemen and an ambulance took him to hospital where he was treated, luckily, for just cuts and bruises and then discharged. Our man finally reached home and entered the house looking like a wounded soldier with plasters all over his chops. He related his sorry tale to his caring wife who replied, 'That's terrible luv, but you were so lucky to get away with only cuts and bruises. By the way, did you bring in an evening paper luv, I want to check last night's crossword solution?' Our man is well known to have plenty of 'north and south' (mouth) but in this instance he was totally at a loss for words!

I recall another one of the regulars relating his terrifying experience last year. He was heading along the Perimeter Road on his way to T4, when he heard this thunderous roar overhead and looked up to see a massive plane no more than 10ft above his head. The plane, as we all know from the media coverage, crash-landed well short of the runway after it lost all power in its jet engines. I remember the cabbie being interviewed on telly soon after the event and I couldn't help noticing he was still wearing his bicycle clips!

Then there was the cabbie who was driving west up the A4 late at night and noticed a Jumbo Jet in his rear-view mirror, getting closer and closer to the ground. The Jumbo came ever closer and ever lower until, suddenly, it seemed to abort and gained height again. At the following inquiry it was said that the pilot wasn't familiar with Heathrow and had mistaken the lights on the A4 as the runway lights and was preparing to land on it. Even more bicycle clips required!

8

THE FAMOUS LONDON TAXI SHELTERS

The London taxi shelters have been an integral part of our trade as far back as 1876. Even the night drivers who work at Heathrow invariably finish their shift with a visit to one to enjoy a nice hot meal. The shelter in Pont Street, the one in Knightsbridge nicknamed the 'Bell and Horns' (named after an old pub that used to be nearby and sited opposite the V&A) and the 'All Nations' in Kensington seemed to be the most popular with the airport boys in my day. The popularity of a shelter was often enhanced by the nearby presence of a toilet and, in the old days the one in Pont Street had one almost attached. It was one of the lovely, dark green old-fashioned, cast-iron loos erected by the God-fearing Victorians with no roof and completely exposed to the elements. We cabbies nicknamed them 'the Iron lungs' and I can distinctly remember many of these walk-in loos were sited at many major junctions all over London at one time. Now they've almost all been demolished, including the many public conveniences built underground. Can't you remember as a kid seeing the magic glow at night from the underground lights through the quartz glass? The councils decided to close all these down as well, but the real reason is unknown. The one at Shepherds Bush was first to go after a well-known actor was charged with indecent offences. My local loo on Hampstead Heath owed its demise to a world-famous performer performing dubious acts, closely followed by the loo on Islington Green, again involving a well-known face. All this raises the pertinent question, where does the modern-day man/woman now go to perform his/her natural functions? Incidentally, I find it totally unacceptable that many of these public conveniences in London are now perceived by some local councils, not as 'conveniences', but more as nice little earners! One of the worst offenders in trying to eradicate the 'public' from the 'convenience' is Westminster City Council that attracts millions of visitors to their world-famous historical sites every year. They have imposed a staggering 50p charge on most of their gentlemen's conveniences, so in effect we're talking 50p a pee! I can sympathise a little if the council is directing its profit-making scheme directly at tourists – even though, with the benefit of hindsight, it may well backfire on them. But these exorbitant charges are a financial burden on the 24,000 London cabbies who transport these tourists to the various sites and require these facilities many times daily – especially the more mature ones with sensitive bladders! Maybe they could instigate a fair scheme where London cabbies, on production of their badges, could qualify for a free pee or even a 'cabbie's special discount'!

But I digress. Unfortunately our particular 'Iron Lung' in Pont Street turned out to be a popular meeting place at night for the local aristocracy who had probably learned their fetish at public schools. This in turn attracted some of the young guardsmen from the nearby Knightsbridge Barracks trying to subsidise their meagre pay. Most of us cabbies adopted the attitude of 'I'm not bothered as long as they don't give me grief.' But not so one of the airport boys who was an out-and-out homophobe; in fact, Sid 'Vicious' – as the boys called him behind his back because of his violent temper – was a racist and a xenophobe as well! He didn't like black people, he didn't like foreigners and he hated bloody 'iron-hoofs', cockney rhyming slang for 'poofs'! I've told this story before in my regular columns in the trade press, so at the risk of being accused of self-plagiarism, I'm telling it again because it's so hilarious.

Sid 'Vicious' turned up late one night and decided to visit the 'Iron Lung' before having his supper. On entering he noticed a shadowy figure lurking in the corner, so he dashed next door to the crowded shelter and burst in shouting angrily, 'There's a bleeding poof next door and I'm going to do him good and proper.' His anger was aggravated even more when one of wags remarked, 'Didn't he offer you enough dough, Sid?' This snide remark almost turned Sid into some sort of demented soul and, grabbing the shelter keeper's heavy steel bucket full to the top with 'tea grouts' (this was well before the introduction of tea bags), he flew out of the door. The next thing the boys heard was a loud thud and a sickening scream of pain. Sid had lobbed the bucket into the roofless 'Iron Lung' and presumably on to the head of the unfortunate guy who Sid thought was doing a bit of 'cottaging' on the quiet!

Sid 'Vicious' returned with a smile of satisfaction on his face and took his usual seat. A minute later the door burst open and in came a guy, wearing a very-expensive looking camel hair coat that was covered from head to foot in tea leaves. This created even more laughter until the guy pulled out his warrant card and yelled, 'What no-good bastard did this? I've been sent here by my nick to check out some of the gay goings-on and this is all the thanks I get for it!' We managed to placate the Ol' Bill with a cup of tea and convince him that it must have been a local weirdo who despised gays!

Incidentally, the 'All Nations' shelter gets its nickname from the immensely popular Great Exhibition of 1851, masterminded by Prince Albert and held just behind the present site of the shelter, in Hyde Park. While on the subject of Prince Albert, I must tell this hilarious story of a recent tour I did with these two little old American ladies. I had just started the tour from a Kensington hotel and immediately stopped outside the Albert Memorial to start my chat. I informed them, knowingly and in my best thespian voice of course, that Queen Victoria and Albert were very much in love and had had nine children. Sadly, Albert contracted typhoid and died within a week at the age of just forty-two. There was a deafening silence in the back of the cab and I imagined the two little old ladies were so touched and humbled by my 'performance' that they just couldn't speak. Not so, as a minute later I heard one of the ladies say to the other with baited breath, 'Gee forty-two kids, that's an awful lot!' For sure I knew they were a bit ancient, but I didn't realise they were a bit 'mutton' (Mutt and Jeff – deaf)! The rest of the tour was taken up with elaborate hand signals!

Another tour – again with two dear old American ladies – proved hilarious. I picked them up at their Bayswater hotel and they must have been studying a map of London, because one of them said to me in a heavy, Southern drawl that made me think of sitting outside a white-painted plantation house, sipping mint juleps and watching the sun go down on the old Mississippi, 'Look-ee here honey, we wanna go past the three plantations and up along the pond.' I stopped to think about her directions for a few seconds before realising that she meant going past Hyde Park, Green Park, St James's Park and along the Thames. But that was far from the completion of their wishes. Once again the heavy, Southern drawl, as she put her head near the partition window and said pleadingly. 'Listen honey, this is our first time in little ol' London town and we'd just love to see one of your royal family. And honey,' she went on, 'we would give you one hellava big tip if you can manage that for us Southern Belles.' I smiled to myself as I headed down Park

Lane towards Hyde Park Corner. I didn't have the heart to tell them that I had been pushing a cab around the streets of London for donkey's years and I had never, ever seen one of the royals. So I just nodded and said I'd do my best.

I turned left into Constitution Hill and as I approached Buckingham Palace, a very large copper suddenly appeared in the middle of the road with his hand in the air. Now, being an experienced London cabbie, I know for a fact that the police view us as an easy nick. Had I been speeding, or was I driving dangerously? I thought to myself in a blind panic. But I was worrying unduly because it was only the royal limousine preparing to come out. I turned nonchalantly to the ladies in the back and said, as though it was an everyday occurrence, 'If you look out of the offside window you will see Her Majesty the Queen and the Duke of Edinburgh.' I thought for one minute that the cab was going to capsize as, following loud screams of excitement, they both rushed over to the offside window waving like mad to the royal couple.

I couldn't keep pace with the massive Rolls-Royce as it glided down Birdcage Walk, but the ladies in the back were in seventh heaven – and I had sent them there. You wouldn't believe it, but as I got nearer to Horse Guard's Avenue on the left, I noticed a wine-coloured Rolls-Royce coming down to the junction and showing the royal flag. Yet again another large copper came into the road and stopped me and yet again I turned to the ladies and said nonchalantly, 'If you care to look into that wine-coloured Rolls-Royce on the nearside, you'll see the Queen Mother and the heir to the throne, Prince Charles!' I never realised, until I looked behind, that mature 'Southern Belles' wore such large bloomers!

I seemed to recall hearing on my radio that the royals were opening some sort of classical music programme at the Royal Festival Hall and we were lucky enough to be passing at the precise moment they were heading there. But I didn't let on to my passengers and I didn't let on when they gave me a ridiculously big tip at the end of the tour. I didn't even let on when they asked for my address so they could tell all their friends back home that whenever they visited London, I was the cabbie who, 'Could show all the English royal family in just one tour!' As the Yanks are fond of saying – I'm your man!

Yet another interesting link with the present taxi trade, Prince Albert and the Great Exhibition of 1851 was the very beginning of the dreaded 'Knowledge of London' that every single licensed taxi-driver in London has to endure before he is considered 'a fit and proper person'. The story goes that Sir Richard Mayne, the then Commissioner of the Metropolitan Police, had received many complaints from visitors to the Great Exhibition that London cabbies didn't know their way around our great capital. So the aforementioned gentleman devised a vast array of 500 routes that criss-crossed all over London, plus hundreds of points of interest that cabbies must know. These 'points' included theatres, railway termini, gentlemen's clubs, hospitals, schools, police stations and just about any other 'point' one could think of. The dreaded 'Knowledge' was born!

This scheme was then handed over to the Public Carriage Office, our controlling body, and they instituted a system where the would-be cabbies attended an oral test every month. The 'Knowledge', which has been compared to the work-rate of a three-year degree, is essentially a process of elimination and persistent hard work. You religiously learn all the 500 or so routes on your scooter – or 'runs' as we call them – making sure you take in all the 'points' on the way. But a warning, don't be tempted to just sit in the comfort of your own home simply map-reading, because the examiner will soon find out and he'll have your balls! Hopefully, and with a bit of luck, he will eventually ask you one of the 'runs' you know on your monthly 'appearance'. After some considerable time, you whittle down the 'runs' and, after answering them correctly, you are granted a 'reduction' from four weeks to three. These 'reductions' slowly go down to an 'appearance' every week until finally you are told that it's time to do your 'suburbs'. This really is a few weeks of map-reading to find your way out to the suburbs. Just one more test before you can receive your coveted green badge, the driving test, or 'the Drive' as we call it.

Finally, the big day arrives; the day that you've been striving to achieve for some three years or more, through ice and snow and wind and rain; the day you proudly receive your badge and 'Bill' (your cab licence). It may well be some forty-six years since I received my badge, but that day will live in my memory forever. I will never forget dashing off to Marcantonio's Café', just along the Lambeth Road, and showing all the other Knowledge Boys my proud possession, then jumping into MY cab and heading for my first fare at Waterloo station. As per usual, my story has got a funny ending. I was hailed by a gentleman in Kennington Road and asked to go to the Continental Club in Tottenham Court Road. Much to my total embarrassment and after all the many hours I had spent learning London, I didn't know this particular club! And all these years later I still don't know where it is! I explained to the passenger that I was a new boy and that the practice – presumably to give you luck in the future – is to give a 'freebie' for your first fare as a cabbie. I dropped him off in the middle of Tottenham Court Road and he walked off quite happy with his 'freebie'!

After all that hard and unpaid labour, it's no wonder that London cabbies perceive themselves as the most professional and the most highly-trained in the world. And it's no wonder that they are somewhat miffed that the PCO seem to favour the 53,000 newly-licensed private hire drivers and try to put them on an even platform with us – or even attempt to integrate us! We licensed cabbies have had to suffer three long years or more of hardship roaming the streets of London, yet the PH driver simply applies for a licence and he's up and running, doing basically the same job as we are! The only difference is that the PH driver has to be pre-booked and he's not allowed to ply for hire, although this doesn't seem to bother the many hundreds of illegal touts roaming the West End late at night! Many of the wise old heads in our trade believe the PCO should be divided into two different sections as soon as possible, one section dealing with the 'pros' and the other with the 'amateurs'!

Most tourists visiting our great city – and many Londoners come to that – haven't got a clue as to the purpose of the cabbies' shelters. During my many tours of London that I do every year, I have asked my passengers, 'Do you know what those little green huts are?' Because they ARE green and many of them are close to green spaces, they invariably think they are somewhere the Royal Park's gardeners can keep all their tools safely locked up! The long and interesting history of these taxi shelters is well worth recording. The story goes that way back in 1875, a certain Captain Armstrong, who lived in very posh St Johns Wood and was editor of the *Globe* newspaper in Fleet Street, sent his manservant out into the raging blizzard to engage a cab to take him to his office. He waited impatiently for over an hour for his man to return with a cab and asked him why he had taken so long. The manservant, soaked to the skin, replied that although there were cabs on the rank, all the cabbies had retired to a nearby grog shop in an effort to get warm and shelter from the blizzard. Captain Armstrong never realised that London cabbies in those days had to work under such appalling conditions. They were expected to 'sit on the box' in rain, snow, wind and cold, just waiting in hope of a fare. No wonder many of them found solace in the day by nipping into the local grog shop and fortifying themselves with mugs of cocoa – and maybe just a wee nip of rum!

The good captain spoke with many of his influential friends about the fact that cabbies had simply nowhere to shelter from the elements. Being God-fearing Victorian gentlemen, they all sympathised with the poor cabmen and decided to donate money for the erection of London's first taxi shelter adjacent to the cab rank in Acacia Road, St Johns Wood – very convenient for the good Captain Armstrong! These donations were placed in a trust and named the London Cabmen's Shelter Fund. Many wealthy and influential people – including the Prince of Wales, later to become King Edward VII – subscribed to the fund. One particular shelter, erected in Old Palace Yard, Westminster, was paid for by members of both houses of parliament, with the list of subscribers reading like a page from *Debrett's Peerage*! In the early days the shelters had no provision for supplying meals and the cabbies just used to sit there, quite happy to be out of the cold, eating their sandwiches and having some sort of liquid refreshment. By 1882 larger shelters were erected which included a small kitchen, with hot meals being served by the shelter keeper both day and night.

During the next seventy-five years, some forty-seven of these shelters were erected at the larger taxi ranks in inner London. Sadly, due to new one-way systems at Marble Arch and Great Portland Street and the Piccadilly underpass, not forgetting Leicester Square becoming pedestrianised, they have drastically declined in numbers. The shelter that stood in Leicester Square for many years was lifted up, placed on a lorry and re-sited in Russell Square where it stands to this day.

Harking back to the Leicester Square shelter reminds me of back in the 1960s when it was frequented by many regular

Heathrow night drivers. I recall one little clique that were all young, East End Jewish lads and they had this fascinating way of working a cab. All through the summer they would work their socks off and then they'd work right through and over the Christmas holidays and New Year's Eve, which was always a good earner in the past. But the following day they were off to the Canary Islands until Easter. What you have to remember is the Canaries hadn't even been discovered by the package-tour companies in those far-off days and, I don't think they even had an airport! So the lads made their way to London Bridge where the banana boats used to moor and off they'd go. I can remember one of them telling me that you could live comfortably on five shillings a day – especially if you got on friendly terms with one of the many ladies spending the winter out there, possibly living it up on their late husband's insurance payout! So not only were they enjoying the sun and the sea, it was also a bit of 'tea and sympathy' as well! I loved listening to their tales when they arrived back all nicely tanned, some three months later. In fact, as a young husband with two children, I was quite jealous at the time! Mind you I was a bit of a package-holiday trail blazer in the 1960s and well remember travelling to Lanzarote in the Canaries with my wife in the very early days. We had a bumpy landing on arrival and were ushered into what only could be described as a large Nissen hut that served as a terminal at the newly-built air strip. The look on my wife's face was one of utter disgust at my choice with a boiling hot wind blowing in from Africa and the tumbleweed bouncing uncontrollably against the old Nissen hut. She finally said, angrily, 'Where on earth have you bloody brought me?' I had to agree, the beaches had black sand from the volcanic lava, the countryside was like a lunar landscape and every tourist was invited to go up the volcano on a camel, no less, for their big kick. No, I'm sorry, not for us.

So the next year I chose Benidorm, which in those far-off days was still a fishing village. Again I got a rollicking because we had gone in the winter and the whole place was like 'Geriatrica-on-Sea', with all the thousands of pensioners completely taking over the town and enjoying the balmy winter weather on the Costa Blanca. Mind you, I did get a couple of good offers! Not to be put down, the following year I booked a package holiday in Malta. It wasn't a good year for the Brits going to Malta because their left-wing Prime Minister Dom Mintoff disliked the Brits so much, he had thrown all of our troops off the island. So my wife and kids 'enjoyed' a quiet time in a holiday complex that catered for over four hundred people. However, because of Dom Mintoff's alienation of the Brits, there was just my family and twelve other lonely souls on the complex! From that very day to this, if I wanted a holiday I had to go with the boys on golfing trips. My wife said 'enough is enough'!

But back to the taxi shelter and, thankfully, those remaining thirteen shelters are now refurbished regularly by English Heritage and have been made Grade II listed buildings. So whatever happens in the future, these taxi shelters will live on as a lasting memory to the longevity of the famous London cabbie.

I thoroughly enjoyed the camaraderie in many of these shelters during my twenty years of working nights. Sadly, the great characters that frequented these shelters – both cabbies and the odd celebrity or two – are no longer with us. In this day and age of tight security and smoked-glass limos – plus the intrusion of the Paparazzi – you could never hope to pick up a genuine celebrity in your cab, let alone sit alongside one in a taxi shelter! It wasn't like that in the 1960s and '70s, especially working on the radio circuits. You would get sent to the BBC Television Centre in Wood Lane and pick up the likes of Sammy Davis Junior, the recently departed Eartha Kitt and any number of world-famous performers who had come across to star in *Sunday Night at the London Palladium*. A frequent night visitor to Pont Street was the once-beautiful Ava Gardner, the ex-Mrs Frank Sinatra. I found it quite sad to see the downward spiral of a once-famous and beautiful film star. I don't know if it was the booze but she had got very fat and just sat in the corner drinking her coffee and having a fag. The boys took it in turns to take the wobbly lady back to her home in Ennismore Gardens.

When the shelter door opened late at night – especially in Pont Street where all the celebrities stayed – you just wouldn't believe some of the famous faces asking for a cab. Many of the top American stars favoured the nearby swish Carlton Tower hotel and I recall Henry Cotton at the door, Jack Palance and Prince Aly Khan, the son of the Aga Khan and husband to the beautiful, Hollywood star Rita Hayworth. All I can remember was this handsome, Indian-looking guy, very smartly dressed in a white tuxedo, asking politely for a taxi to take him to the Embassy Club. The shelter was full and all the guys were eating their grub and one of them told him to get a passing cab. What happened next was pure theatre. Prince Aly Khan pulled out his wallet and extracted a white fiver – that shows how long ago it was. He held the white fiver in the air and said somewhat theatrically, 'The first gentleman to finish his meal will receive this.' Nevermind the old saying about 'women and children first', this white fiver constituted the best part of a night's work and any woman or child unfortunate enough to be in the shelter at the time would certainly have been crushed to death in the ensuing stampede! One of the guys told me later that it was in fact one of the airport boys who received the 'goodie'!

Sadly in today's modern world where everyone is flying about at a hundred miles an hour, many of the new, and for the most part younger, cabbies don't frequent the shelters as we did back in the 1960s and '70s. With big mortgages and expensive taxis to pay for – either renting or buying them – many of these new drivers just crack away eating their sandwiches and drinking their flasks of coffee while parked on ranks! It wasn't at all like that in the old days because most of us were 'on the clock' and you kept the tips and paid a percentage in to your guv'nor. Then, one bright garage owner came up with a new scheme in the 1970s, renting out cabs on 'the flat'. That meant paying your guv'nor a set sum every week and keeping the cab all the time. This guaranteed your guv'nor a guaranteed sum, thus eliminating the popular fiddle of 'Stalking' – that's working without having the meter engaged, preferably late at night! So no longer did all the guys have to pay in after a day or a night's work and no longer would they gather at all the garages and have a nightly chat with their mates. Consequently, many of the night fitters lost their jobs, as did the guys who ran the night-drivers home in the early hours of the morning. It's getting so tight financially in the shelters today that one of the lady shelter-keepers informed me that without the local builders queuing up daily for their cups of tea and bacon sarnies, they would soon go out of business! That's a strange scenario don't you think? Back in 1875 the Victorian philanthropists took pity on the poor old cabmen and generously donated money to build them forty-seven taxi-shelters to protect them from the elements. Now, some 135 years later these remaining shelters are being kept open, thanks to the regular custom of Polish builders! Call me an old dinosaur if you will, but I find that a sad reflection on the once-famous and renowned, but now largely defunct camaraderie of our great trade.

9

MY TAXIS

When I first got my badge just before Christmas 1962, I needed to get on the road as quickly as possible because I was short of dough after all those months on the Knowledge. There was a small cab garage near my home and I managed to persuade the guv'nor to let me take one out. It was the height of a freezing cold winter and my ancient FX3 was almost as cold inside as it was outside! The FX3 had a single driving compartment and an open luggage space alongside, but the wind used to whistle though the badly-fitting, sliding glass window.

I recall one incident with the old cab that still makes me chuckle today. I was hailed by a Jamaican lady in Camden Road, who had quite obviously never been in a London taxi before, because she proceeded to climb into the open luggage compartment. I informed her politely that she was allowed to sit in the back because she was a paying customer!

The cab was certainly nippy, but it had one serious drawback: the old-fashioned rod brakes. Whenever you needed to stop a bit lively the FX3 had the nasty habit of pulling to the left or the right, but as you got to know the vehicle you were able to take the appropriate action. That explained the note left on the windscreen written by a previous cabbie which read, 'she pulls to the right, so go left-hand down.' Another strange feature of the FX3 was the four internal jacks that you could crank down to the floor from the driver's compartment in the case of a puncture. This was a great innovation, unless of course you were leaving a boisterous taxi shelter late at night and one of the wags had cranked them down without your knowledge. So you would get into the cab, start her up, put her into gear and go absolutely nowhere, with a crowd of your mates doubled up with laughter. This prank was usually reserved for the new boys, or 'Butter-Boys' as they were known!

I decided after working for a garage for a couple of years, to buy my own cab. I fancied one of the snub-nosed Beardmores, a solid, coach-built vehicle that was very popular with all the drivers, especially when they introduced the new, four-door model. So I duly ordered one, but just as I reached the top of the waiting list, they went broke and ceased trading. After my initial disappointment, I then decided to buy one of the new FX4s that had come on to the market in the late 1950s. Incidentally, the FX4, along with the Mini, became the longest-lived of British car designs with an eventual lifespan of thirty-eight years. From 1959 to 1997 there were some 75,000 FX4s produced.

I duly made an appointment and went to Mann & Overton in Wandsworth Bridge Road – in those far-off days the only taxi distributor in London – to order my new cab. The offices and the staff in M&O's had to be seen to be believed; they were something else and in another world. Their waiting room was adorned in dark oak panelling with faded pictures of old taxis and former directors on the wall, almost out of the Victorian era. As for the staff, talk about being snotty-nosed. Even the receptionist looked down her gold pince-nez at me as if I was something she had removed from the bottom of her shoe and not a valued customer. Okay, so there was a waiting list for the FX4, but I was still going to spend around £1,200, a lot of dough in those days.

I was escorted up the oak-panelled stairs by 'snotty-nose' and ushered into an even grander office and greeted indifferently, this time by a snotty-nosed man. This was followed by the normal questions about my finances, my ability to pay back the HP money, any extras I would require on the new cab and so on. Finally, I signed on the dotted line and I was now the proud owner of PJD 288E which I could pick up in the front garage. I can always fondly remember driving out of the garage and picking up a fare almost immediately. I well remember the fare as well, although not so fondly. She was an attractive young lady with a bloody great dog on a lead and, before I could say, 'I don't carry dogs except Guide Dogs,' this hoofing hound jumped up the side of my pristine cab and scratched the paintwork!

My next cab was called an FX4R and this one was a waste of space, it couldn't accelerate very well and was incapable of climbing up the hill to my home at the top of East Heath Road. In fact, I used to tell the funny story of two coppers on a bicycle, and a milk float, overtaking me. Apparently Carbodies of Coventry, the makers at that time, had purchased a shipment of new engines from India that were hopeless! Next came the FX4 Fairway, an excellent and reliable vehicle that is still going strong today.

After reverting back to working for a garage for a few years, I then bought myself a Metrocab, which I still drive after some twelve, trouble-free years. What I liked about the Metrocab was its fibre-glass body that wouldn't rot with rust like the Fairways. When the company started making the TTT I put my order in and, yet again they went bust before I reached the top of the waiting list. I could never understand the reasons for them going bust because the TTT was a cab well ahead of its time design-wise and is still very popular today.

Finally, we come to the latest model, the TX4 – well out of reach of my pensioner's pittance, but hugely popular with the young cabbies who don't bother too much about 'miles to the gallon'. All through the years many of the younger drivers have been crying out for an alternative cab that's not so expensive or looks so old-fashioned. The stumbling block facing all the vehicle manufacturers who wanted to enter the lucrative nationwide taxi market has always been the stringent Conditions of Fitness laid down by the Public Carriage Office. The condition that stipulated a 25ft turning circle would mean re-tooling all their assembly lines, certainly not an economic option. Then, quite recently, along came Mercedes and with typical Teutonic cunning their engineers devised a quite simple plan to bypass this impasse. They created a clever system where, at the touch of a button, the rear wheels would engage as rear-wheel steering, thus being capable of completing the necessary 25ft turning circle.

The authorities were compelled to allow this procedure because it passed the condition laid down. So Mercedes fitted this rear-wheel steering – plus a few other taxi features, to their Vito and started flogging them as London taxis. Again this created many differences of opinions about the new Vito. The trade organisations welcomed them as alternative vehicles and say that in time it will bring down the price of the TX4 and compel LTI, their manufacturers, to offer a better service and a better deal to their once-captive market. The cabbies who drive the Vito say they are great and attract many lucrative out-of-town tours, while the cabbies who don't like them sneer and call them 'Bread Vans'. My take on this situation goes a bit deeper. My concern for the future of our trade is the scenario of too many alternatives. What is to stop all the other car makers from buying the Mercedes patent and flooding the market with alternative taxis? Back in the early part of the nineteenth century there were some thirty-eight different makes of taxis, yet within a few short years most of them had gone bust.

At the risk of being called an old dinosaur – and not for the first time I might add – I believe the 'recognition factor' is absolutely vital if we want to retain our status as 'world icons' and, with various alternative taxis possibly roaming the streets of London in the future, I honestly don't believe we can achieve that. Our passengers – especially the business people – feel comfortable with our 'recognition factor'. When they hail a licensed taxi they expect a knowledgeable driver and a completely passenger-safe vehicle that will protect them should they ever be involved in an accident. Whether any of these alternative vehicles will ever match that standard, I simply don't know. I've written literally millions of words over my forty years of being a trade journalist, warning about the impending dangers the trade faces from unlicensed minicabs. And I've written literally thousands of words warning about the eventual licensing of these vehicles. Nobody took much notice of my warnings then and I doubt whether they will take much notice this time around!

10

HEATHROW ON 7 JULY 2005

Nobody can ever forget that terrible day of 7 July 2005 when a gang of young, British-born Islamic terrorists attacked London because of Britain's role in the Iraq War. At 8.50 a.m., three bombs exploded within 50 seconds on London's underground network, followed at 9.47 a.m. by another terrible explosion on a number 30 bus in Tavistock Square. Fifty-two innocent commuters were killed and some 700 were injured. The first bomb was detonated on the Circle Line underneath Aldgate, the second below Edgware Road station and the third at King's Cross, deep underground. It was the deadliest attack on London's transit system in history.

I was out working on that fateful day and my suspicions were aroused by various broadcasts on the radio about a 'power surge' on the underground network and talk of 'serious electrical problems'. My suspicions were further compounded when I discovered my mobile wasn't working, the reason being that the whole mobile network had collapsed because of the many thousands phoning their loved ones with reassurances after the explosions. Suddenly there weren't any buses on the streets anymore and hordes of people were seen queueing up outside shuttered underground stations. It was just as manic out on the streets with people desperate to find cabs and it seemed like the perfect opportunity to earn bundles of dough. But I just wasn't happy with the situation in London, it didn't seem right and I couldn't understand why. So my instincts got the better of me and I packed up work after a few hours and went home to my terrified wife. She had heard the latest news of the outrage and was worrying like mad about me and my son Nick, also a London cabbie.

That was in central London, so what was happening out at Heathrow Airport? Some months later I was involved in a major TV documentary series called *The Iconic London Taxi* and it was my job to interview many of the guys at Heathrow about that fateful day. The testimony of Jimmy Smith, the LTDA's senior rep, who had inherited the job from me, bears witness to the dedication and bravery shown by many of the regular cabbies at Heathrow. What you need to remember is nobody was quite sure if there hadn't even been bombs planted at Heathrow – especially in the tunnel. Consequently, all outgoing flights, bus and underground services were cancelled as a safety precaution, but the long-haul fights were still arriving with their passengers. That left just the dedicated London cabbies to clear the thousands of stranded people from outside the terminals – plus a horde of illegal touts who descended like vultures for the pickings and proceeded to charge exorbitant rates. The area could well have been booby-trapped as a prime target, so these cabbies were taking a chance by continuing to provide an essential service for the stranded passengers.

I'll quote Jimmy Smith to describe the manic scene on that terrible day:

> Once we realised what had happened in town, we organised all the trade reps and taxi marshals to control the masses of people on all four terminal ranks and we sent out a 'Code Red' message to all the radio circuits. This meant all taxis to head straight down to the ranks, bypassing the taxi feeder park. What we attempted to do to clear the rush

> was to 'marry-up' individual passengers who were going into London into groups of five. These were loaded into taxis and quoted a reasonable set fare for each person. Even those going to places like Windsor, Bagshot, Egham, Camberley and towns in that general direction, were also rounded up together in an effort to eke out our supply of cabs that weren't sufficient for our needs. As the day progressed and, as more cabs in town discovered that it was 'in and out' at Heathrow, our complement of cabs started to improve. The trade reps and taxi marshals supervised the ranks all through the day and late into the night – with just the odd tea break – until finally we got all the passengers away.

He added that he thought the reps, taxi marshals and the cabbies did a marvellous job under very trying circumstances and, without the cabbies, the passengers would have been trapped until such time as the public services opened again. My sentiments entirely, even though some cynics might be saying that the cabbies earned an awful lot of money in just one day!

While on the subject of dedication and bravery, I must re-tell the story of a very brave cabbie who is a regular at Heathrow. Mike O'Leary was a sixty-six-year-old grandfather at the time of this incident (March 2000) and was quietly tootling back empty to the airport down the M4. He noticed a four-door saloon car driving slowly on the hard shoulder, the car's left indicator was flashing but the vehicle was slowly edging out right and into the middle lane. Mike pulled past the car and, from his high vantage point in the cab, he saw that the driver had collapsed with his head leaning back on the seat. By this time the slow-moving car, obviously still in gear, had reached the middle lane and was moving erratically into the fast lane of the now-busy motorway. So Mike quickly parked his cab and dashed across to the middle lane in the hope of stopping the car, which was moving at about 10mph. Despite the screeching of many horns and motorists yelling out that he must be 'effing mad', Mike managed to pull open the front passenger door and, holding on to the central partition with one hand, jumped into the car and fell in a heap on the floor. Mike managed to knock it out of gear and applied the handbrake. Trouble was, the car was a hazard parked in the fast lane and after making sure the guy was still breathing, Mike got out to direct the traffic, while phoning for an ambulance. As luck would have it, another motorist with knowledge of first aid stopped and tried to resuscitate the guy. Even more luck was to follow when a passing ambulance noticed the incident and the paramedics took over. Thanks to Mike's undoubted bravery and the help and quick response from others, the motorist survived a major heart attack. Which all begs the question, what makes a hero? Are we all born brave, or do we suddenly become blindly brave in a desperate, life-threatening situation? With the greatest respect to Mike, he was a most unlikely hero – his days of racing down the right wing and using his fast-footwork had long gone. However, in my humble opinion, his outstanding bravery – with no regard for his own safety – certainly deserved a bravery award from our government. For sure Mike's story has been told on TV quite a few times and they at least appear to appreciate his courage. And, I know from sources that he actually gave his TV fees to the recovering heart attack victim. Not only brave, but generous as well! What really gets up Mike's nose is that the government still refuses to give him an official bravery award which he so richly deserves. Their latest excuse, after Mike had obtained the help of his local MP to lobby Gordon Brown, was that the incident happened too long ago. I find that rather strange when they are still giving out posthumous bravery awards to heroes of the Second World War whose stories have just come to light!

11

HEATHROW'S FIFTIETH ANNIVERSARY

Back in 1996, Heathrow Airport became fifty years old and with the massive PR opportunities afforded by it, BAA was determined to make a big splash. The queen had already accepted an invitation to open the massive refurbishment of Terminal 2, so they thought they could kill two birds with one stone and ask her to open the fifty-year celebration display on the same day. This she agreed to do.

First job for the organisers was to select a site big enough to house all the stands. The Visitor Centre on the North Side of the airport – almost adjacent to the taxi feeder park – was the obvious choice. Next job, to try to get a cross-section of all the many people and companies involved in making up the day-to-day running of the airport. And that's when our co-operative, Heathrow Airport Licensed Taxis, was invited to take a stand. As chairman at the time, I thought it the perfect opportunity to advertise our trade in full view of the 'great and good'. So I started chatting-up all my major advertisers on the *HALT Magazine* for sponsorship, to help pay the wages of the guys operating the stand for at least a week. Obviously the added bonus of a royal appearance made the cost of any advertising well worth the money and many well-known names agreed to come on board. I had already requested that the organisers site us by the back door, suitably placed by the car park where, I hoped, we could put our taxis on show. Thankfully they agreed and when LTI (London Taxis International) put up their sizeable chunk of advertising dough, they also agreed to my request to send some new – and some old – taxis to put on show.

The stage was set and the big day had arrived. Our guys had been working like mad to put on a good show on our stand; the cabs had arrived on low-loaders and were lined up outside our back gate. All the dignitaries had assembled, awaiting the arrival of Her Majesty and I can always remember Steve Norris, the then Minister of Transport for London, coming up to the stand and addressing me as 'Alf' in a very friendly manner, despite the look of amazement on some of the faces of his entourage that the minister was calling a common cabbie by his Christian name. It was no big deal really because we had spoken before at meetings about the trade and about the possibility of abolishing the entry charge to the taxi feeder park. I can remember the minister informing me at those meetings that just as soon as HALT had all four taxi desks up and running, he would seek to abolish the charge. Sadly, by the time we had achieved this, Steve had been replaced.

The fact that we were sited right at the back by the rear exit didn't bother me too much. Okay, so we wouldn't be on centre-stage for the TV cameras, but the car park for our taxi display was essential to show our 'wares'.

Suddenly, a couple of hours before the arrival of the royal visitor, there was sudden flurry of movement at our end and a group of smart, dark-suited guys with suspicious-looking bulges in their jacket pockets, came to peer out of the of rear gate. Apparently the top-brass weren't too happy with the supposedly high security risk at the front entrance and they were looking for a safer alternative for the sovereign. Within a short while, everything had changed and now we, formerly the 'back-door Johnnies', were now the 'front door Kings' and the very first to be seen by Her Majesty. The big boys who had paid mega bucks for a stand near the front entrance must have been as sick as pigs, while we, who had paid 'buttons', were now at centre stage!

So the organisers had to change everything around in double-quick time. The hordes of kids with their Union Jack flags, courtesy of BAA, were hastily shepherded around to the back and stood in two lines making a funnel-like entrance. And all the bigwigs – including the PM and many other famous politicians, were busy adjusting their ties outside our stand. Finally the queen's limousine pulled up alongside our cabs. She was greeted by the bigwigs as she strolled past our cabs, giving them an interested look. The Duke of Edinburgh – who actually owns a green Metrocab, so he can be transported around the capital without being recognised (the same colour green as my Metrocab in fact) – stopped to give the cabs a long, hard look. Our stand was the first Her Majesty saw and she gave Colin Evans and myself a friendly smile as she moved on with her entourage. So by sheer chance we had cracked it and our royal exposure was worth every penny to our loyal advertisers!

Most of the rest of our day was spent trying to control the hordes of kids – and parents – fiddling about in our borrowed taxis. The kids were loving it, sitting in the brand-new taxis and blowing the horns and switching the indicators on and off, while their parents sat in the back seats with big grins on their faces. I reckon we attracted more wannabe taxi drivers on that particular day than Ken Livingstone's later plans, as Mayor of London, when he offered the ethnic minorities all sorts of freebies to do the Knowledge in his effort to break what he allegedly termed as, 'The white mafia that permeates the London cab trade.'

After a long, hard day it was along to the refreshment bar to enjoy a nice cup of tea and a bite to eat. Then, as the day drew to a close, we all went outside to enjoy the spectacular fly-past by the Red Arrows, flying in V-formation alongside the mighty Concorde. Who would ever have thought that a few short years later this mighty plane, the world's very first supersonic airliner and technically way ahead of any other passenger aircraft, would be heading for the scrap yard because it was considered to be uneconomical? The tragic crash and loss of life outside Paris's Charles de Gaulle Airport, was also a PR disaster for the French Concorde. Nevertheless, I am of the opinion that decisions had already been made to axe it before the crash.

Heathrow's fiftieth anniversary celebration was a great day and one never to be forgotten. But more to the point, it was also a great PR scoop for the taxi trade at Heathrow. We had shown by our presentation and our cab display, to both the dignitaries and the public alike, that our trade was an integral part of Heathrow and could stand alongside all the major companies and still make an impact.

12

THE ART OF BEING A SUCCESSFUL CABBIE

Driving a cab in London is a unique profession. You leave home maybe in the early hours – or at lunchtime, or in the evening – with just your 'float' of small change in the cab. You're on your own and it's entirely up to you how much you can manage to earn in a shift. If you are renting a cab from a garage, chances are you need to take the first forty-odd quid to pay for the cab and the diesel. It really is a lottery; you can turn right to start work and have a bad day, or you can turn left and have a good day. A word of advice from an 'old timer' for the new guys and gals coming into the trade, never ever start your shift with a money target in mind. Looking for a set sum of money can be soul-destroying, very stressful and over a period of years can lead to heart problems. Let me set the scene. Unfortunately, for a variety of reasons, on some days and nights, it's simply dead on the streets of London and if you're unlucky enough to be caught out there desperately trying to earn enough to pay your mortgage or your rent, then it can become a veritable nightmare. Take my advice and just plod away until it's time to go home.

Whether we like it or not, it's a proven fact that we cabbies benefit from the misery of others. If the rain is hammering down, there's a strike on the tube, the buses or the rail network, or the ice and snow have caused the signals to fail, then the volume of taxi fares not only increases considerably, but the actual distance of the fares dramatically increase as the poor old, long-suffering commuters attempt to make their way to and from work. Obviously we don't want terrorist attacks to happen, or death and injuries to innocent people, but when these emergencies sadly occur we are normally the only transport facility in the whole of the capital still operating. Without us, all the long queues at airports, stations and bus stops would never be cleared up. Okay, so cynics may be saying that we are making bundles out of the misery of others, but hey that's real life and, as in real life, things even themselves out over the three months of the 'kipper season' when it's deadly quiet out on the streets. Incidentally, this expression dates back to the Victorian era when during January, February and March, it was so quiet out on the streets that all the poor old cabbies could afford to feed their many children with was cheap kippers!

Many cabbies with astute business acumen – especially those who have succeeded on the much-coveted Blue-Badge Guide Course – including many of the airport regulars, have set up their own websites. I know from my late daughter that passing this guide's course is possibly as difficult as doing the Knowledge. She attained a degree in Russian at Brighton University and became one of the few Russian-speaking, London tour guides until the dreaded breast cancer took her from us in 1999. But I'm happy to say that her loving husband Keith has just been presented with his Blue Badge diploma, so her wishes live on.

These guys and gals advertise their guiding skills on the internet and attract advance bookings from many tourists coming to London from all over the world. After an exchange of e-mails they invariably finish up meeting their passengers at Heathrow or one of the other London airports and bringing them back to their central London hotel.

Obviously this creates an immediate bond between the customer and the tour-guide cabbie that often lasts for their complete stay. More often than not, the cabbie spends the whole week taking them to Windsor, Hampton Court Palace, or as far afield as Stonehenge, Bath or Stratford-upon-Avon. A return trip to one of the airports completes a very successful week for this cabbie – with the added knowledge that these tourists will certainly pass on word of his services to their friends. And that, my friends, is the successful art of cabbing!

My decade of working at Heathrow regularly in the 1990s, plus my political involvement as LTDA senior rep and later as chairman of HALT, meant that I needed to get back to the airport for various meetings. As I mentioned in an earlier chapter I filled in various forms and paid my dough for an Airbus taxi licence that allowed me to pick up at all the Airbus stops without touting for passengers. Some days I would manage to get a cab-full, other days just one or two punters, but it was certainly better than going out there empty. Now it was time to learn the art of becoming a successful Heathrow cabbie by giving out your business card to each and every punter for a possible tour – or even the return journey. But to be really successful there were many more wrinkles to learn. My most profitable ploy was firstly to ask my three- or four-hander where they were eventually bound for after I was asked to go to one of the main-line stations. Sometimes it was Birmingham or Dover, or even Bournemouth or Southampton. Then I would proceed to estimate the train fare per person to this destination, finally adding on the taxi fare to this particular station. Invariably the combined fares of all three would add up to three figures and I would quote a price close to that to take them directly to their final destination, saving them some two hours extra travelling time. That old adage is particularly true, 'You win a few and you lose a few.'

My greatest pleasure was to pick up American tourists at Heathrow who had never been to London before and, even though I must admit that I am not a qualified Blue-Badge guide, I do sub-contract regularly with Black Taxi Tours and have some forty-six years experience of London's most famous landmarks. I start chatting to them early on as we head for the Park Lane Hilton and ask if they would like me to point out some places of interest on the journey into town. The reply is always a very responsive, 'You betcha Al!' The first point of interest comes immediately after you cross the Chiswick flyover as there on the right stands a pretty, white-painted cottage. At the start of the eighteenth century, this pretty cottage stood by itself in a deserted field a couple of miles from Chiswick Village and was given as a present by Lord Nelson to his illegitimate daughter Horatia. She was the result of his scandalous affair with Lady Hamilton.

Crossing over the traffic lights at Sutton Court Road we see the grand entrance on the right of Chiswick House followed by Hogarth House, once the home of the famous artist of the same name. I quite often need to explain to my passengers that back in those days this whole area was farmland wending its gentle way down to the River Thames.

Some tourists, especially Americans who tend to open their mouth before their brain is properly engaged, get rather confused at some of the great ages of the buildings found in England. I remember once when I was attempting to give a tour of Windsor Castle to half-a-dozen dear old American ladies. After I had finished my 'inspiring' talk I asked if there were any questions. One of the old girls said quite seriously in a deep Southern drawl, 'Lookee here honey, why did your queen build her lovely palace so near to Heathrow, it's so noisy!' Exit Alf stage left with egg on face!

Then it's over the Hammersmith flyover, showing them the final route of the boat race on the right. However, explaining the boat race is a totally different matter as they cannot understand why just two teams should be in the race with one guy remarking laconically, 'So at least one of them will get second spot, Al!'

Undaunted I carry on down Cromwell Road and show them the blue plaque on the right where the famous English film director Alfred Hitchcock lived for many years. That went down well anyway as the Yanks fondly remember him.

Now we are approaching one of the most beautiful areas of London, called affectionately in memory of Prince Albert, Albertopolis. First up is the amazing Natural History Museum in all its terracotta-brick glory, many of which include images of plants and animals. Many of my past passengers have often asked if this was Buckingham Palace and it really is that staggering if you take the time to study it. The architect who first started this build in the early nineteenth century was called Captain Fowke, but sadly he died in 1865 and the build was taken over by Alfred Waterhouse. It's still known locally as the Waterhouse Building. Whether you are a tourist or London-born, it's well worth a visit with or without your kids.

I tell my passengers that I am going to turn left to miss all the heavy Knightsbridge traffic and I immediately point out the magnificent Victoria and Albert Museum on the right, known by most people as the 'V&A'. The origins of the V&A date back to the Great Exhibition of 1851. In 1854 it was transferred to its current site from Somerset House and renamed the South Kensington Museum. It was officially opened by Queen Victoria in 1857.

Next up on the left is the Science Museum designed by Sir Richard Allison and opened in stages from 1919 to 1928. I told my passengers that this is a 'must' for both kids and adults. The Imperial College is the next building on the left. Founded in 1907, it is possibly the most famous engineering college in the whole world.

The last building on the left before entering Hyde Park is yet another Victorian masterpiece: the Royal Geographical Society, with carved statues outside of all the famous explorers of the time including Doctor Livingstone. I have to tell my passengers about my recent adventure into this stunning building. I had been invited to give an hour's talk on my books to the ladies of the Chelsea and Kensington American Women's Club. I duly arrived with my wife and was ushered into the beautiful marble lounge where the ladies were running some kind of raffle. After some coffee and biscuits I followed the 'boss-lady' down some more beautifully marbled stairs to, would you believe, a complete theatre with a stage, stalls and a balcony. For sure I had given many talks in the past at various locations, but none as grand as this. Around 250 ladies listened to my talk and formed an orderly queue afterwards to purchase signed copies of my books. This story brought looks of admiration from my passengers and I reckoned I could flog them some of my books!

I cross over into Hyde Park and point out the marvellous, gold-embossed Albert Memorial on the left. There's an interesting story about that embossed gold and how it was painted black during the First World War. Apparently some bright spark at the War Office believed that the shining gold might reflect on to Kensington Palace for the German Zeppelins to bomb. That's a bit far-fetched don't you think? After all, the airmen in those days were literally just chucking the bombs over the side! Nevertheless, the memorial remained painted black for the next eighty years until a couple of million pounds was raised to restore it to its original beauty in the 1990s; it was officially reopened by the queen in 1998. After her beloved Albert died suddenly of typhoid in 1861, a distraught Victoria had commissioned the memorial and it was designed by Gilbert Scott. The memorial was unveiled by Queen Victoria in 1872 having taken ten years to complete.

I turn right into the South Carriageway and point out the eyesore that is the Knightsbridge Barracks, home to the Household Cavalry. Only the War Department could ever get away with building such a monstrosity on beautiful parkland! Down to the end of the road and out through the Queen Mother's Gate into Park Lane North. Just one more historical site to point out, just look to the right and you'll see Apsley House, the home of the first Duke of Wellington and his descendants. They gave it to English Heritage to preserve, with the family and their descendants able to live in the top flat, free of charge forever. My passengers were suitably impressed when I informed them that the postal address of Apsley House, because of a tollgate situated outside many years ago, was 'Number One London' – how grand is that?

Finally, at the end of the journey and my mini-tour, they, hopefully, say how much they have enjoyed my talk and, after giving out my business card, some even ask if I'm available for a tour the following day? I tell them that if they fancy a day's tour of Windsor, Hampton Court Palace, or any other historical spot, then I'm their man. No hassle, no prices mentioned, I just tell them to look up the prices per person for the coach tours of these areas, then to give me a ring and I'll better the given prices.

The outcome with one group was that I carried these Americans all over the country for the next ten days and finally took them back out to Heathrow. Their friends phoned me the following month and some more friends the month after that, booking my services. So, being pleasant, polite, knowledgeable and, dare I say witty, can get you a good living without having to trawl the empty streets of London. Apart from the dough, I thoroughly enjoy showing visitors our wonderful city. I think this is yet another classic example of the art of being a successful cabbie!

13

THE THREAT FROM THE HEATHROW EXPRESS

Even before the fiftieth anniversary plans had been put into place, we were hearing on the grapevine of a major scheme that BAA had signed in 1993 in partnership with the Great Western Railway's board. If the reports I had been hearing about a direct express line from Paddington to Heathrow were in fact true, then it could well decimate much of the passenger-base our trade had painstakingly built up over many years.

Further down the line it became a proven fact as the Heathrow Express was under construction and due to open in 1998. BAA was putting up most of the money – around £350 million – with Great Western Railway allowing the use of their main-line tracks as far as Hayes – for a fee of course. Most of the staggering cost would be spent on tunnelling some 5 miles underground from Hayes, under the Spur Road and into the three terminal stations – now four with Terminal 5 up and running. Strangely, no station was ever built at Terminal 4.

From the very start, the Heathrow Express was unique compared to any other rail line. Because it was being built with private money, BAA had somehow managed to persuade the then Tory government that it shouldn't come under the auspices of the Rail Regulator. That meant, in effect, that when it was finally opened they could hike up the fares whenever they thought fit to do so, or make special deals. In fact, it could do just about anything it wanted to do at any given time with no redress from anybody.

Once again our trade had missed a God-sent opportunity. We had all known for years about the oncoming threat and we had had plenty of time to formulate a competitive pricing structure and to start setting up a local rank system. Even way back before construction had ever started, we met with the then BAA Managing Director Mike Roberts and he more or less told us what the future would be for the licensed trade at Heathrow. I'll quote what he said to me verbatim, 'I see the future of licensed taxis at Heathrow as being in the periphery of the airport.' In effect what he was saying was that with the arrival of the Heathrow Express, we could well be restricted to mainly local fares. However, once again internal politics reared its ugly head and the various warring factions couldn't agree on what most intelligent people perceived at the time as a perfectly workable local rank system put forward by HALT. The trade farce became even more farcical some three years later when the original vociferous opponents of the proposed local rank at the time, presented an almost identical system! Yet still, these people insisted that 'their' system was a totally different concept from HALT's and had been approved by 'the majority in the canteen.' By then the 'Sleeping Giant' hadn't woken up in time and, as is the regular failing in our trade, we had missed the boat yet again!

Despite the well-documented and serious massive collapse of the tunnel under Terminal 3 which resulted in a major hold-up on the construction – and a final bill of £440 million – in 1998, amid a blaze of publicity, our most formidable and most expensive competitor was up and running.

Not too many years later, in June 2006 to be precise, despite objections from every quarter, BAA was taken over by the giant Spanish company Ferrovial. It's a strange old world isn't it? Back in the early post-war years our government perceived

BAA – or its forerunners – as possibly the most important of all British companies. That's why they went to such great pains to nationalise it. Now, some four decades down the line, it has been flogged off to a foreign buyer!

The Heathrow Express was scheduled to run from 5 a.m. until midnight for seven days a week, at fifteen-minute intervals. The distance was around 16½ miles and would take some sixteen minutes to Terminals 1, 2 and 3 and another five minutes to Terminal 5. There would be two dedicated platforms for the express at Paddington and the opportunity to travel this short journey by Business Class – for a little extra of course.

The next obvious step for BAA was to pull out all the stops in order to market and expand their massive investment worldwide. Their first marketing venture was to sell tickets through their UK travel shops, followed by travel shops all over Europe and the USA. They linked the ticket sales with promotions via package holidays, free trips to stately homes, or freebies on the London Eye. An obvious selling point that they targeted was the sale of return tickets at a slightly reduced rate, so the punters were safely 'locked up' both ways! Another advertising ploy they adopted and, as a dyed-in-the-wool supporter of our trade, I never ever dreamt would work, they somehow persuaded the big fleet owners to put Heathrow ads on the sides of their TAXIS! I know that money speaks all languages but come on, this must be a classic example of the trade shooting itself in the foot. At the very same time that the trade organisations at Heathrow were madly busy trying to protect the livelihood of thousands of cabbies at the airport from the threat of the Heathrow Express, you have this crazy scenario of many cabbies in town advertising the opposition with slogans like, 'Fifteen minutes from Paddington, the quickest way to get to Heathrow.' And the farce didn't end in town because I often used to see some of these taxis carrying this ad in the taxi feeder park! However, as far as remonstrating with these drivers and hoping to get a sensible reply – forget it. All I got was, 'I only drive the cab mate and I don't know what's on the side and, to tell the truth, I ain't really bothered.' I wrote an article in the trade press on this particular subject and asked why it wasn't possible for our trade organisations to come up with an advertisement to stick on the sides of taxis, extolling the virtues of a licensed taxi to Heathrow. I suggested something like, 'Two or three passengers in the back of a taxi is the cheapest – and quickest – way to get to Heathrow,' but, as per usual, nothing came from my suggestion.

After the Heathrow Express became operational I thought the initial fare of £10 for a single second-class ticket was a bit pricey for a journey of just 16½ miles – especially if you equate it with the fare at the time on the Gatwick Express. I believe this fare was about £11, but, this was for a journey almost 10 miles more than the distance of the Heathrow Express. However, because this was a privately funded enterprise which had managed to get the nod from the government, it was able to do what it wanted and when it wanted. The Rail Regulator which controlled ALL the franchises on the then British Rail was said to be frustrated with this scenario, but they were powerless to do anything. So, consequently, the single second-class fare crept up to £12 for a single journey within a few short months. This was in fact good news for us cabbies because by this time, the regular passengers arriving at Heathrow had come to realise that BAA's slogan plastered all over the terminals reading, 'Just fifteen minutes into downtown London,' wasn't quite right. In fact, you certainly couldn't call Paddington station 'downtown London'. It didn't take the punters too long to come to the conclusion that three people at £12 each makes £36, plus a cab at Paddington for around £10 equals £46 in total. So, by sharing a cab into the West End, they would in fact, not only be quids in, but also get there more directly and certainly quicker! It was the same picture for the cabbies in town; three or more people sharing would get to Heathrow quicker and cheaper by cab and without having to hump their luggage in and out of stations. Most of the regular cabbies at Heathrow, including myself, were pleasantly surprised to see many old faces return to riding in taxis. It appeared at the time that the initial novelty of the Heathrow Express – plus the aggravation of trying to get a cab at Paddington in the morning and evening rush-hours – was wearing a bit thin.

Sadly, it proved to be a false dawn for our trade because with such a massive investment of private money spent on the Heathrow Express, it couldn't possibly afford to fail. Even so, over the last decade the fares have continued to shoot up every year and in 2009, the price of a single economy fare was a staggering £16.50 and the return was £32. However, it's the price of the business class fare that fascinates me. Who on earth would want to spend £26 for a one-way ticket and a massive £50 for a return on a short, fifteen-minute journey?

I recall many years ago when the underground network eventually reached Heathrow, all the 'doom and gloom merchants' were predicting the end of taxis at the airport. That didn't happen, though, after passengers discovered to their cost that stopping at more then twenty tube stations and taking well over an hour to get into central London just wasn't economic if you were a business person. So once again they returned to riding in taxis.

Exactly the same scenario occurred in 1998 with the opening of the Heathrow Express, but thankfully HALT and many of the more intelligent cabbies have had – out of necessity – learned to adapt to the new situation. Credit cards were now the prime order of the day and possibly the 'currency' of the future at Heathrow. Quite simply, if you don't carry a swipe card supplied by the many sources – for a small percentage of course – then you've got to be some sort of dummy because you will lose out. Today's modern business person who wants to get to somewhere – say in the Midlands urgently – and requires a taxi is certainly not going to be carrying £200 in 'readies'. So, no credit card facilities then no long fares!

The latest figures from the Heathrow Express (2009) show they are carrying a massive 15,000 passengers every day and that Paddington station is without doubt the busiest station on the whole of the UK rail network. Even the taxi rank at Paddington must hail as the longest of all the taxi ranks anywhere in the world, but it moves all the time. Thankfully some trade bodies in town have got themselves organised – especially the LTDA. They supply a team of taxi marshals at the station every morning from 7 a.m. to 10 a.m., five days a week, to operate a shared rank system in an attempt to clear some of the massive queues. The marshals go down the queue offering fixed-price cards to those who want to share and the shared rank has proved very successful with the travelling public, the cabbies and station management alike. I know many cabbies who are on the rank bright and early and sometimes manage four shared rides, equating to the best part of a day's takings. The marshals also try to help out people, mostly foreigners, who haven't got an inkling of where they are or where they want to get to. This is just the sort of innovative thinking that will keep our trade on top over the coming years and certainly one that could be easily copied at Heathrow. I am well aware that HALT are operating a taxi marshal scheme at Heathrow, but presently this is purely on a voluntary basis. In effect the guys offer their services for a couple of hours instead of just sitting in the canteen or the taxi feeder park. What the trade really needs to eliminate the accusations of unfair practices, are fully-paid taxi marshals – similar to the guys on the taxi desks. But again it's all about the ability to finance a scheme such as this. However, full-time and fully-paid taxi marshals working a full shift could and would generate many extra fares in the future.

Strange to relate and despite the ever-increasing threat from the Heathrow Express to our passenger base, the latest throughput figures from the taxi feeder park (2009) also show a substantial increase of taxis passing through over eighteen hours. These figures indicate the massive increase in air travel over the past decade and the stats for the future indicate a further 20 per cent increase over the next decade.

So does that mean there's more than enough fares for everyone and that we as a trade at Heathrow can just bumble along as we always have in the past? Not a bit of it; the guys and gals out there need to be vigilant and united. The biggest threat for them in the future as I see it, are the ever-growing numbers of minicabs – now known as licensed private hire. Many of these companies have got major backers and major finance. It wouldn't take rocket science for them to obtain a print-out of the taxi numbers passing daily through the feeder park, then calculate some 3,000 fares at an estimated 'x' number of pounds equals an awful lot of dough. Even now, my sources tell me, they are bidding for booking desks in all five terminals and this will be followed by requests to park their vehicles as taxis are allowed to do. In today's modern business world, sadly, moral obligations do not enter the equation. If the PH proprietors offer BAA a sizeable sum for the use of parking facilities, then BAA will certainly investigate any potential sites on the airport. And, if there are no sites available, what's the betting that they won't utilise one of the taxi feeder parks?

Our sixty years of loyal service to the airline passengers counts for nothing, it's all about money. We presently share the PCO with private hire whether we like it or not. We also share the SGS facilities (a private company to whom all the overhauls of London taxis are outsourced) with them when we go up to get our cabs passed for their annual overhaul and we have to lump that as well! What are the odds that we won't be sharing something 'out west' with them within the next decade – and possibly the canteen to boot? Pie in the sky, some may be saying, but I wouldn't bet against it!

14

THE POSSIBLE FUTURE FOR TAXIS IN LONDON AND HEATHROW

By the time this book is eventually published the London Olympics will be just around the corner. These games, I believe, will become the benchmark deciding the future of the famous London cabbie and whether the long and illustrious history of our trade – and our iconic status world-wide – will be enough to survive the ever-increasing threat from private hire.

When Mayor Ken was in office, rumours were circulating from City Hall about the possible shortage of some 10,000 licensed taxis needed to cover the extra millions expected to flood in for the games. Some bright spark in City Hall – possibly with vested interests – was reported as suggesting that because of the so-called 'shortfall' of licensed taxis at this crucial time (incidentally nobody has ever seen the data from this so-called shortfall), then wouldn't it be a sensible idea to permit private hire to ply for hire – only during the games of course? It is crazy suggestions like these from, presumably a person who is *au fait* with PH and has been duly elected to City Hall, that could endanger the future of our trade. If ever PH were allowed to ply for hire during the

London Olympics, or at any other time come to that, then some other bright spark on the payroll would immediately congratulate everyone on their foresight and say, 'If it worked once, why not try it out every Saturday night when cabs are hard to come by, or even every Bank Holiday when many cabbies are not working?' And that, my friends, if we allowed it to happen, would be game, set and match and a fond farewell to 350 years of licensed taxis! I only hope that Mayor Boris never subscribes to this crazy concept.

What we in the trade need to understand is that many of these major PH companies pay out big bucks to employ lobbyists to reach 'the great and the good' in high places, including City Hall, the Houses of Parliament and BAA's top management. The bottom line is, if your project could be worth millions to your company in the future, then it's well worth your while to pay out the thousands up front!

Even as far back as the late 1950s it was alleged that Michael Gotla, the brains behind the launch of Welbeck Minicabs which was to threaten our very existence, had major financial backing from a millionaire businessman and had at least three MP's on his payroll to lobby the tabloids and ask questions in the House to further his cause. An article in *The Times* on 2 March 1961, obviously written by someone on the Gotla payroll, was quoted as saying, 'Men of wealth have been heard to cry out against the taximeter – men who think nothing of signing away many thousands in seconds at the wiggle of a pen, but find it painful to sit helpless in the back of a taxi watching their money drip away in three penny stages.'

All very graphic and dramatic, but this journalist seemed blissfully unaware of the fact that sixty years back his paper had been in the van for the introduction of the taximeter. I believe the bosses of all the tabloids chipped into the kitty way back in 1907, to help with the prize money for the winner of the workable meter competition. This competition was mooted after the London General Motor Cab Company of Brixton, with the biggest fleet in London, refused point blank to put their fifty brand-new Renault cabs on the road because they reckoned the devious cabbies were fiddling them – how dare they! No way would they allow their massive investment to be compromised without the invention of a workable meter. And the winner of the contest – just out of historical interest – was a German nobleman called Baron von Thurn und Taxis. He called his meter a 'Taximeter' and we've been known as taxis ever since! It's rather weird that some fifty years later the introduction of another fleet of Renaults on to the streets of London – this time unlicensed minicabs – was to pose a serious threat to the longevity of the licensed trade for the next fifty years!

With the benefit of hindsight, Gotla's three MP's earned their corn in the House because the government decided in their wisdom that operating a pre-booked, radio 'taxi' service wasn't counterproductive to the very stringent Hackney Carriage Laws. Therefore, they deemed the project as legal. The Home Office also washed their hands of the matter, sharing the view of the government that minicabs were simply an extension of the private hire trade and, as such, were to be welcomed by giving the travelling public another option. But as events continued to unfold, it became blatantly obvious to all and sundry that there were those on the scene who were determined to see that the law was abused for their own benefit. Despite the Hindley Report of 1939 and the Runciman Report of 1953, which both clearly defined the law of plying for hire, the government continually stated that plying for hire had no statutory definition which made it difficult to obtain any convictions. Inevitably, Welbeck Motors, with its massive expenditure on staff, radio equipment, the cost of all their cars and smart uniforms for drivers, soon went bust. By 1965 a petition for its compulsory winding-up was issued with a total liability of £50,000!

However, the end of Welbeck Motors certainly wasn't the end of the minicab scourge; it proved to be just the opening of the floodgates and the beginning of an ongoing, fifty-year threat to the licensed trade. Gotla had exposed, for all to see, the gaping loopholes in the private hire laws and those loopholes were still there to exploit. Many shrewd and powerful people were sitting patiently in the wings, watching while the Welbeck scenario reached its inevitable conclusion. The game plan had been clearly revealed. All they had to do, when they chose to enter the ball-game, was to get their strategy and figures correct – unlike the unfortunate Mr Gotla – to ensure maximum profits in the future!

Consequently, over the next three decades the numbers of unlicensed and uncontrolled minicabs continued to proliferate across London. It seemed that every street in Soho and every street in south London had these tatty minicab offices on show. But this time around the big-money boys who ran these seedy premises had done their research well. Unlike Gotla, who had splashed out enormous sums to supply all the Renault Dauphines, these guys simply provided the radios and the jobs – at a price of course!

It has to be said that we as a trade didn't do too much to halt this minicab expansion. We cabbies wrongly believed that achieving our green badge after many years of hard work, gave us carte blanche to just sit and watch.

It was inevitable that some sort of control had to be put on these many thousands of often unroadworthy vehicles, with drivers of questionable records. Even the big operators in the PH trade were crying out for some sort of legislation because the bad press were putting their own businesses at financial risk.

The inevitable happened and the minicabs – now called by the upmarket name of private hire – were finally licensed and within a few short years their numbers had escalated to a frightening 53,000 – more than double the number of licensed taxis. In the meantime, many London cabbies were still living in the past enjoying the demise of Welbeck Motors and wrongly believing the minicab threat was over. In effect, over a period of nearly half-a-century, our trade didn't do too much to counter this ever-increasing threat to our livelihood. Okay, so we took a few of the touts to court and many of the dedicated ones turned up for the demos – while other cabbies carried on working – but not much else. Not so the opposition who busied themselves by investing heavily in radio equipment, drivers and new premises. At the time I wrote vociferously in the trade press that we should copy the method used by the French cabbies when they had a difference of opinion with their government. They would ALL go out on to the streets of Paris in their cabs, get out, lock the doors and simply walk away. After just one day of complete traffic gridlock, the authorities wanted to talk. The Heathrow cabbies reading these facts may well be saying to themselves, 'So what? It's all very interesting, but nothing to do with us because it's only happening in town.' Don't kid yourselves guys and gals, this rapid escalation of our opposition will, in time, spread its tentacles all over London and eventually reach Heathrow.

I like to play Devil's Advocate because it's a great way to access any forthcoming possible scenario. Firstly, if I was a marketing man for a PH company, I would build up a solid customer base in town, then move into the corporate market and slowly undercut the licensed radio circuit's lucrative account customers. In the old days, the big City account holders wouldn't touch minicabs with a bargepole. But now they are *kosher* with a much posher title, that makes for a different ball-game! It would appear from the latest news that the PH companies are winning the battle for the lucrative City accounts and that the licensed radio circuits are suffering a big downturn in their corporate business. Sadly, for the future of our trade, some of them have gone for the easy option of colluding with the opposition and, in one case, actually buying into a PH company of their own. According to the chairman of the circuit concerned, in his recent report he made this ludicrous statement, 'It can only be of benefit to the licensed trade in the future.' Apparently the new buzz-word in this latest scenario is, 'a one-stop shop', which basically means that a licensed radio taxi circuit should – in his opinion – be able to provide its customers with a taxi, a car, a limousine or a van. Not only are these elected people, who haven't been behind the wheel of a taxi since the old queen died, threatening the very fabric of our trade, they are also introducing an invidious atmosphere between the hundreds of drivers on the radio circuits and the many thousands who aren't. I question many of my friends who are on the 'radio' and ask them why they don't walk away if they don't like the 'minicab policy' that has been foisted upon them. Their answer is a sad reflection of the modern-day cabbie's thinking when they say, 'We've been fighting them for nearly fifty years and haven't won, so I reckon it's time we joined them!'

My next major step forward – and something the grapevine tells me is already happening – would be to 'lock-up' all the major hotel chains in central London by offering set-price deals for their guests to all the four airports or elsewhere. This would appeal to the hotel chains because certainly they would receive a small sum in 'appreciation' of their compliance and a car would be waiting readily outside for their guests. The poor old cabbies sitting on the hotel ranks would eventually be reduced to just doing the local fares that PH don't want. I could name half-a-dozen top West End hotels that already operate this system, but still some of the 'brain-dead' continue to rank up outside their premises. Subsequently, if these PH drivers picking up airport fares are worth their salt, they will surely chat up the punters for any possible return journeys, which in itself will reduce the amount of fares for the airport cabbies. How many times have you been sitting on a central London hotel rank and seen one of the out-of-town cars pick up a fare? Simply multiply these scenarios many hundreds of times when their operation reaches Heathrow and only then will you begin to realise that, 'yes, it really has got something to do with us!' I know it's an old-fashioned saying but it really is true, 'the cake is only so big.' In point of fact, the PH operation is already up and running in and around the vicinity of Heathrow. They have latched onto one of HALT's original proposals from way back in the 1990s that was dismissed at the time by the volatile dissenters. We wanted to introduce a fixed-rate fare to and from all the local hotels, thus generating more work when it was quiet, but it was knocked-back by the dissenters who refused to pay the hotels a commission on each fare. Now PH have got contracts with all the hotels local to Heathrow and the fixed-price fare is a whopping £18 – with the hotels taking six quid from every fare. Just imagine the extra volume of work that would generate for us during this recession!

Let's assume, rightly or wrongly, that within the next decade private hire have got a firm grip on the City's major accounts and most of the big hotels are doing a deal with them; what next? Again playing Devil's Advocate, the next obvious step would be to make inroads into the lucrative Heathrow taxi customer base. Firstly set up your stall in all five terminals and, as long as you pay the going rate, BAA will do business with you with no moral obligations. Now your business is prospering but you need somewhere to park all your vehicles. The licensed taxis have their own feeder park and as a good paying customer, then why shouldn't BAA grant you the same privileges? If you look at it from their side, it's a valid argument. BAA will argue that there's simply no more space on the airport for all these private hire vehicles, but the shrewd operators – after having done their homework – will reply, 'But the taxis have two feeder parks. Surely you can find some room for us sharing with them – at the going rate of course?' Again a valid argument if you look at it from their point of view.

All of these thoughts in my mind are purely hypothetical, but could well become a reality in the future. We are facing an opposition numbering twice as many as us, and the Public Carriage Office, at the present time, are not even treating the licensed trade as equals. All the many taxi-orientated senior people at the PCO have long since retired and been replaced by young staff who are basically career managers. They perceive their duties as just being part of Transport for London and don't have any affinity whatsoever with us, the professionals. In fact many of them wrongly believe that there's no difference between the two trades under their control. It doesn't concern them one iota that we've sweated blood for three years or more to gain our green badges. If they consider that a ruling may favour private hire, so be it if that's the wish of TfL. A recent classic example of their muddled thinking – and one that provoked probably the biggest demonstration ever by London cabbies – was their involvement with Westminster City Council to allow an illegal rank to be set up at night near Leicester Square for the use of private hire vehicles and their 'Clipboard Johnnies' touting outside the clubs and bars. They are well aware – as are Westminster City Council – that it is illegal for any private hire vehicle to be seen in a public place and to be seen to be offering a service. Yet they totally ignored the advice from our trade leaders and went ahead with the project anyway. Yet still they insist that this so-called 'minicab rank' is perfectly legal. This is one battle we can ill afford to lose.

This muddled thinking could well reach Heathrow in the not-too-distant future if the PCO start to liaise with the airport owners. BAA are not great lovers of 'bolshy' taxi-drivers, they have had to put up with us for the past sixty years out of necessity. But things could change very quickly if big bucks were offered to them as an inducement for 'services rendered' to private hire. BAA own all the land on the Heathrow site (to be precise, they lease the land from the MOD) so they can rent it out to whomever they please. At the risk of repeating myself, if they deem fit to rent space in the terminal buildings to PH desks, they will, and, if these PH desks start advertising reasonable set price fares all over the country, then they will. And, if BAA want to earn more dough by renting part of the taxi feeder park to PH for the going rate, then they will! And we, as licensed drivers, will simply have to put up with it.

So, apart from saying we're, 'Up the creek without a paddle', where does this possible scenario in the future leave the licensed trade at Heathrow? First and foremost the trade MUST be united, with every single man and woman belonging to some trade organisation. What concerns me at this present time are the numbers of trade organisations out there. We have the LTDA, HALT, Unite (formerly the T&G), the LCDC and lately HATDU, all pushing for their own agenda on behalf of their members. I've just heard that HALT, which I helped to form, is calling an EGM in the hope of changing from a co-operative to a society. This will enable them to change the rules, reduce the quorum to a realistic 20 per cent and vote in new executive members. I wish them luck in their venture which could result in bringing satisfaction to their membership.

Then, in the middle of all these trade organisations, you have the majority, those who don't belong to any of them, yet are quite happy to enjoy any negotiated benefits. Unfortunately, if you have five different trade organisations sitting around the same table with BAA, unless they've agreed a game plan before, it will be a total waste of time. If a strategy has been agreed before any meeting, then it makes sense to elect just one person to speak on behalf of the trade. But knowing Heathrow politics that will never happen although maybe, just maybe, there could be change in the water.

In July 2009, BAA dropped a veritable bombshell on the trade at a monthly meeting by informing them, out of the blue, that they would be running a six-month experiment allowing minicabs the franchise for all advanced bookings in Terminal 3 and Terminal 5. It's a well-known fact that British Airways is losing many millions of pounds during this recession – in fact, they are more affected than most other airlines, especially the budget airlines – the main reason being that they have always made their profits from Club Class passengers paying well over the odds for their flights. Now, during this recession, those passengers are either travelling economy or, in many instances, not travelling at all. So now BAA is desperately searching for ways of making money. They have conjured up this scheme – for the right price of course – allowing minicabs to take away all the rightful fares from the licensed drivers who pay £5.50 every time they enter the taxi feeder park.

Addison Lee, London's biggest PH operator, was given the franchise for T3 and One Transport was given T5. It was no surprise to see Addison Lee in the forefront as they are well known for their aggressive marketing policies; I have a sneaky admiration for their acute business acumen. However, the involvement of One Transport was a shock to everyone, because this is a subsidiary of the Radio Taxis Group which is a licensed taxi circuit with hundreds of cabbies as subscribers. This was the final proof – if any more was needed – that the board of RTG didn't give a damn about the trade and were only interested in making money for their shareholders and at the expense of licensed drivers. It's sad to think that this radio circuit was set up as a friendly society in the 1950s by a group of dedicated cabbies for the benefit of other cabbies. Sadly they were persuaded by a 'Pontius Pilate' and his henchmen to de-mutualise because the shares would make a nice pension. Now the shares are worth about as much as Italian lira and the company is in a deep spiral. As one of my fellow trade journalists said succinctly, 'The subscribers on RTG must feel like turkeys voting for Christmas!'

So the battle-lines were drawn with everybody in the trade realising that this 'six-month experiment' could well signal the demise of the licensed trade at Heathrow. BAA weren't too concerned about crossing swords with the FIVE trade organisations as they knew from past experience that the internecine squabbling would still continue. However, on the day of 'the showdown meeting', somebody had thought up a master stroke (I believe it was a request from Mick Rose of the LCDC) and asked the Rail, Maritime & Transport Union's Eddie Lambert to send along one of the big guns to support the trade. And along came Bob Crow himself, the head honcho and militant leader of the RMT Union to speak to the drivers in the feeder park. Now for those of you not familiar with the aforesaid gentlemen, he's the boss-man of the RMT Union who regularly bring London to a standstill with strikes on the train and tube networks. You may not like him for his bolshy, aggressive, Arthur Scargill-like manner, but you have to admire him for all the work he puts in for his union.

His appearance at Heathrow soon got back to the airport authorities on the grapevine and had them literally quaking in their boots, because they were well aware of the havoc his union could create at Heathrow. And when BAA were faced with a united trade – at long last – informing them in no uncertain terms that they would be in dispute if the minicab scheme wasn't withdrawn by the end of the day, plus the spectre of Bob Crow waiting in the wings, they quickly 'bottled out' and suspended the experiment forthwith, making waffling noises about sitting down with the trade to improve the taxi product in the future.

In my opinion this is far from the end of the matter because BAA will attempt to introduce some other potential money-making scheme in the future, which will be detrimental to the licensed cabbies. I'm told that many regulars at Heathrow have now joined the RMT and maybe that's the way forward to secure our future. I've always believed unity is the backbone for strength and that under one banner – like the Paris cabbies – our 'gang' of some 25,000 drivers could cause plenty of aggro. I'm not knocking the splinter groups at Heathrow who have flourished from the disenchanted – they do a good job in their own way for their members – but the old adage, 'United we stand, divided we fall,' could not be truer in this instance.

If most of the regulars decided to follow Bob Crow's militant leadership and join the RMT, then I'm certain the BAA wouldn't want any hassle from them and would think long and hard before introducing any sort of minicab service at Heathrow. But the latest news is that the new taxi driver members of the RMT are not at all happy, especially the guys and gals who work regularly at Heathrow. They had to approve the RMT's campaign to install tachographs in cabs and restrict the hours that taxi drivers in London are permitted to work. These working hours would include all waiting times on ranks – including two to three hours waiting at Heathrow! The problem here is that the vast majority of RMT members are employed so it's a very good campaign as far as they're concerned but I think the new taxi driver members have been forced to approve a 'suicide pact' that could threaten their livelihood.

I thoroughly enjoyed my ten years or so of being involved with the Heathrow politics and I think they are a great and generous bunch of lads and lasses. My take on their future is that they badly need dynamic leadership to steer them through the possible troubled waters ahead. They need a person vastly experienced in trade matters and one who has a clear vision of the dangers facing the trade from PH. Last but not least, they need to listen to this person and not the rabble-rousers pushing for their own agenda.

I wish them all the luck in the future – they're certainly going to need it – and as for my hypothetical conclusions, I sincerely hope I am so, so wrong. Only time will tell.